The Things That Need Doing

A MEMOIR

Sean Manning

Broadway Paperbacks · New York

BROADWAY

Copyright © 2010 by Sean Manning

Published in the United States by Broadway Paperbacks, an imprint of
the Crown Publishing Group, a division of Random House, Inc., New York.
www.crownpublishing.com

Broadway Paperbacks and its logo, a letter B bisected on the diagonal, are
trademarks of Random House, Inc.

Library of Congress Cataloging-in-Publication Data

Manning, Sean.
   The things that need doing: a memoir / Sean Manning.—1st ed.
     p. cm.
  1. Manning, Sean.   2. Children of cancer patients—Ohio—Biography.
3. Mothers and sons.   4. Bereavement. I. Title.
   RC265.6.M26 2010
   362.196'9940092—dc22
   [B]   2010007667

ISBN 978-0-307-46324-1

Printed in the United States of America

Design by Level C

10 9 8 7 6 5 4 3 2 1

First Edition

The Things That Need Doing

For Mom

You may well ask why I write. And yet my reasons are quite many. For it is not unusual in human beings who have witnessed the sack of a city or the falling to pieces of a people to desire to set down what they have witnessed for the benefit of unknown heirs or of generations infinitely remote; or, if you please, just to get the sight out of their heads.

—Ford Madox Ford,
The Good Soldier

Average Length of Stay . . . . 7.11 days

—*Cleveland Clinic Heart
& Vascular Institute
2007 Statistics*

Being in a hospital almost every day for over a year was like spending that long in a foreign country. At first, I had no idea what anybody was saying. After a few months, I'd picked up enough essential words and phrases to make do. By the end, I'd become fluent. Once the hospital visits stopped, of course, my tongue lapsed, and in the six months or so that passed before I began writing this, my reversion from eloquent expat to inarticulate alien was near complete. So while I researched extensively to refamiliarize myself with the pertinent terminology, and had the book vetted by doctor acquaintances, understand that this is not reportage. It's memoir—*my* version of the story. I've therefore changed the names of all medical professionals and hospital staff as well as altered certain identifying details. Same with my extended family and friends, out of both respect for their privacy and narrative expedience.

The Things That Need Doing

CHAPTER ONE

I.

I probably should've left early. She even told me to go. The procedure was scheduled for ten the next morning. I'd have to be back first thing. But I wanted to say it right at midnight—or, rather, since by then I knew better than to trust the unit's clocks, at the moment *Home Improvement* ended and *The Fresh Prince* began.

I got up from the high-backed chair and went to the side of the bed. A full-on hug was out of the question; jostling the ventilator hose even the slightest bit was liable to set her off on one of those awful coughing fits. Instead, I delicately slipped my left hand behind her neck, steadied myself against the air mattress with my right, leaned down so that our noses practically touched, and smiled.

"Happy birthday."

She smiled herself, mouthed her thanks, and ran a hand trembling from medication and nervousness about the procedure through my hair. Reaching past my temples, it was the longest I'd worn it since freshman year of college—like my love for basketball, an old proclivity renewed in the eight months since the heart attack and my return home.

I leaned closer still and was kissing her forehead when her nurse came in with the Ambien. (I forget who—being a Wednesday, officially Thursday, most likely Nick, maybe Night Christina.) Before I could step aside and gather my things to go, she clutched my arm. However shaky, her grasp was still plenty strong. She'd quit smiling.

"Don't say anything," she mouthed.

I understood perfectly—she'd be bummed enough spending her birthday in the hospital without the nurses and aides and other well-wishers among the staff popping in every five minutes to remind her of the fact—and so, before finally leaving to go home and grab a little sleep, promised her I wouldn't blab.

Except someone already had. Aunt Claire probably, or maybe it'd been deduced from her chart or wristband. For when I walked back into the room in the morning, there was tied to the nightstand a helium balloon and HAPPY BIRTHDAY! written on the dry-erase assignment board.

Both were Wendy's doing. Of the ten or so respiratory therapists within the Cleveland Clinic's Respiratory Special Care Unit (reSCU), she was the one I knew least. Unlike most of the RTs, whose schedules varied—a morning here, an evening there, and, with no limit on overtime, often both—Wendy worked strictly first shift, from eight to four, leaving about a half hour before I usually arrived. Still, our paths crossed enough to make an impression.

She was around Mom's age, ruddy complected, glasses set low on her nose, heap of blond hair styled in big bangs and a ponytail. As immense as that hair was, her personality was even more so. A world-class talker—five minutes and you'd know the names, ages, and dietary restrictions of her entire family, pets and all—she would have driven Mom batty in better health. As it was, she enjoyed Wendy's monologues. It took her mind off weaning from the vent, and, panicked as that torture justifiably made her, she always felt relieved in the presence of an RT, regardless of whom.

That morning, weaning was of no concern. It hadn't been for a few days now, ever since she'd been placed back on full support—the reason we were finally going ahead with the G- and J-tubes.

Precisely what it sounds like, gastroparesis is the partial or complete paralysis of the stomach. Symptoms range from minor (feeling full quicker) to major (chronic nausea and vomiting). Mom's were major. A gastric emptying test—in which she drank a gray-colored, chalky-tasting barium milkshake, its progress tracked by X-ray—concluded that what would take most people two to three hours to digest took her eight to nine. She was nauseated around the clock and every six to eight hours received medication to help—Compazine or Reglan or Zofran or Phenergan. Less reliable and easy to assuage was the vomiting. She could go three days without, then suddenly throw up every ten minutes for a whole week. Then, just as suddenly, it'd stop. There was no telling why. Suctioning (a thin, vacuuming catheter slid deep into the airway to extract secretions the lungs aren't strong enough to expel and thereby prevent pneumonia) often triggered it, but not always. Three of four different brands of tube feed were tried, but none was better tolerated than the other. The tube feed's delivery rate didn't matter. Twenty cc's an hour—equivalent to four tablespoons—was thought to be safe, but sometimes even that tiny bit would come back up. Whenever it did, whenever any did, the pump would be turned off for a few hours, but that was still no guarantee. The buildup of bile was enough to get her going.

What caused the gastroparesis was no less puzzling. It could've been any number of things—a reaction to medication, something viral perhaps. The rest of the family and I felt sure the bypass had something to do with it, since the nausea and vomiting started shortly after, but the doctors rejected the connection. Their best guess was that the initial intubation following the heart attack or the extubation two weeks later had damaged the vagus nerve, which runs from the brain down the back of the throat and esophagus to the colon and is responsible for initializing digestion.

Pinpointing the cause would've done little good anyway. Gastroparesis can't be cured. Online I'd found a few recent cases in which a newly developed stomach pacemaker had been tried with some success. But the consulting gastrointestinal doctors claimed it was still too untested. Besides, Mom was in no state to endure such drastic surgery. Were the nausea and vomiting to be alleviated, the only viable option was a G-tube.

Short for percutaneous endoscopic gastronomy tube (also known as a PEG), a G-tube is a roughly inch-in-diameter, foot-long piece of pliant rubber sutured to the stomach. Typically used for feeding—a more permanent, more comfortable alternative to the Corpak in the nose—Mom's was to serve the opposite purpose, draining any backed-up tube feed and bile.

That was another issue long in need of resolving: feeding. Because of the extent of the gastroparesis, eating was worthless. The only way she could get any nutrition was from the Corpak advanced through the stomach on into the jejunum, the middle portion of the small intestine.

Some Corpaks can go a couple months before beginning to clog.

Hers was lucky to last half that long, on account of how much medication passed through the pinhead-wide tube over the course of a
given day and how thick and sticky most of it was. (The nurses were
supposed to flush the Corpak with water after every medication and
finished bag of tube feed, but they didn't always remember.) At first,
the clogs were small and could be broken up with ginger ale and a
little back-and-forth on the syringe. For more temperamental clogs,
the Corpak was connected to a gravity bag that was filled with ginger
ale, hung from the IV pole, and left to work for an hour or so before
the nurses tried the syringe again. Before long the clogs would worsen
and could only be undone by Clog Zapper, an industrial-strength
solution that looked like spackling and came in a single-use packet
with its own miniature syringe. When this failed, the Corpak would
need replacing.

For Corpaks that terminate in the stomach, this can be done at
the bedside; because Mom's needed to be advanced farther and into
such an exact spot, she had to travel from reSCU, located on the
eighth floor of the Clinic's G Building, down to the basement, where
the X-ray department was located. Occasionally only a few days
would elapse between trips, such as the time about a month before
her birthday. The Corpak had just been replaced the day before.
Mom was using a tissue to get a hair out of her mouth, a loose corner
of tape snagged the tissue, and, when she took it away, it tugged the
Corpak about a foot out of place. (Total, it was about a foot and a
half long and stayed put via crosswise strips of cloth tape wound
about the tube and the bridge of her nose. Because of how oily her
face would get from not being able to wash, the tape would need
replacing every two or three days. A bridle looped through the nostrils had been tried but was too painful.)

By then—April 27, Claire's journal has it—there had already been talk of the G-tube; following this incident, the prospect of a J-tube was introduced as well.

No different from a G-tube—same dimensions, just positioned six inches or so lower on the surface of the belly—a J-tube is used solely for feeding, directly into the jejunum (hence its name). When the Corpak clogs, it's simply detached and a fresh one is connected to the J-tube. Though the J-tube itself might clog, because of how short it is, it usually flushes without trouble.

While not without potential complications—namely infection— the two procedures were done endoscopically and so were relatively low-risk. The whole thing would take less than an hour. Yet standard as it all was and as much as it'd help Mom, I still had misgivings.

I hated the thought of putting in not just one but two more lines. Already there was the trach, the urine foley, the fecal tube, the peripheral IV in her hand. (Just *which* hand changed daily, sometimes twice a day, and sometimes it wasn't even her hands but her feet, so routinely did the IVs infiltrate, so shot were her veins—the reason the Corpak had to be so relied on for her meds.) For a long time now, with little control over anything except what channel to keep the TV on—and not even that when it came to *Everybody Loves Raymond*—she'd felt like a marionette; more and more she was starting to look like one.

My concern wasn't just cosmetic. Another line meant another port of entry, and that meant further risk of infection. Of course, it was just as dicey not to go through with the tubes, to let the vomiting persist, to run the risk of her aspirating, catching yet another pneumonia, and returning yet again to intensive care. What troubled me more was the way GI had pitched the idea. *All sorts of people have them, people out on the street living totally normal, productive lives. And it's by no means permanent—can be taken out no problem and with only a minuscule scar to show for it.* This was almost verbatim how the trach had first been broached, and, considering how that had panned out so far, the necessity notwithstanding . . .

By far my biggest worry, though, was that once the tubes were in, the long-term-care talk would start up again.

The procedure required that she be completely sedated. This meant placing her on full vent support, for the day at least, possibly longer depending on how sore and fatigued the procedure left her. Lately she'd been making headway weaning. Since that remained top priority, the procedure was temporarily postponed. In the ensuing month she made her most significant progress to date, managing to stay on the trach collar a full week. Then her end tidals (the concentration of expelled carbon dioxide) soared, she was returned to full support, and the doctors went ahead and scheduled the procedure.

Exhausted from weaning, disappointed at being put back on, and nervous about the procedure, she sank into an uncharacteristically despondent mood. Aside from her demands for pain and anxiety meds, that admonition to keep my mouth shut about her birthday was the most she'd said in days. So when I walked into her room and found that balloon and note, I expected her to be livid. She was just the opposite, all smiles, couldn't help being moved by the gesture. It also seemed to ease her fear about the procedure—enough, at least, that she was able to look past it.

"What time's the game on?" she mouthed.

II.

When I was growing up, the Cavaliers played in Richfield, a sleepy village of some three thousand residents midway between Cleveland and Akron. While I rooted my guts out for the Indians and Browns—can still taste the Milkbones our third-grade homeroom ate in a show of loyalty that Friday before 1987's AFC championship—this proximity made me even more partial to the Cavs. So did their living among us—unlike, say, quarterback Bernie Kosar or slugger Joe Carter, mythic figures recognizable only from *Sports Illustrated* covers and Starting Lineup collectibles. Point guard Mark Price worshipped at a megachurch not far from the University of Akron campus. Every now and then you'd catch power forward Larry Nance grocery shopping at the Acme, his head gliding apparition-like above the aisles. When I was nine I scored the autograph of my favorite Cavalier, shooting guard Craig Ehlo, after bumping into him at Tan 'N' Yogurt, a locally owned tanning-salon-cum-frozen-yogurt-shop cashing in on the late-eighties mania for both.

Furthering this familiarity was the venue: the Coliseum. A near-windowless concrete slab surrounded by miles of undeveloped woodland, it resembled a penitentiary, and inside was no less confining. Aisles were few and far between, elbow and leg room nonexistent. Yet the absence of personal space was made endurable by the fact that there wasn't a single bad seat. Even from the upper deck's topmost row you could read the players' expressions. You could hear them, too—their play calling and trash talking and referee lobbying. What's more, they seemed to hear you. I've been to my share of feverishly pitched sporting events, yet have never sensed a team feed off a crowd's noise and enthusiasm as much as those Coliseum-era Cavs. It bound you even closer to them, added to the feeling you were as much a part of their lives as they were yours.

Unfortunately, the Coliseum's existence beyond the bounds of Cuyahoga County wasn't enough to spare its tenants from the inherent haplessness of Cleveland sports, a legacy so fraught with disappointment as to have merited its own lexicon—the Drive, the Fumble, Red Right 88. Beginning with the 1987–88 season, the Cavs advanced to the playoffs six of seven years . . . and were eliminated every time . . . and all but one of those by Michael Jordan's Chicago Bulls, none more famously than in 1989's first-round meeting, in whose fifth and deciding game His Airness sank the gravity-defying, double-clutch buzzer beater near instantaneously dubbed the Shot.

Still, at least they *made* the playoffs.

Following the 1993–94 season, the team picked up stakes for downtown Cleveland. Gund Arena their new home was banally christened, after the team's owner. Unsurprisingly, it wasn't long before I and the rest of the region's adolescent population started referring to it as Gonorrhea. By what I'd later gather from Mom's dinner-table descriptions of the infection, the experience of taking in a game there was only marginally less unpleasant.

Door-to-door to the Coliseum took twenty minutes, and we hadn't needed to bother with the expressway, could just cruise north up sparsely trafficked Riverview Road through the verdant Cuyahoga Valley National Park, all the while catching glimpses of great blue heron and moss-covered remnants of the Ohio & Erie Canal locks and always a grazing doe or two. The hour drive to the Gund required taking charmless, congested I-77, though it too abounded with deer—their mangled carcasses littering the berm and median with almost as much frequency as mile markers.

The arena itself, with its sleek lines and liberal use of glass, should have by rights been more inviting than the correctional-facility-gray monolith that was its predecessor. The Coliseum, however, for all its drabness, was the architectural embodiment of not only the Cavs and us fans but northeastern Ohio as a whole: no nonsense, no frills, a little gloomy, a lot beat-down, but still standing, still with good days ahead. It was something we could all identify with. The Gund was too flashy, too superficial, too expensive.

This stratification was even more keenly felt inside. Though the Gund had only a couple hundred more seats than the Coliseum, there were twice as many luxury boxes, and so the nosebleeds—all my family and friends could afford, as ticket prices had also doubled— seemed miles from the court. Forget binoculars. That high up, nothing short of the Hubble telescope would've enabled you to discern the Cavs from their opponents.

Even then you'd have been hard-pressed. With the move, the team colors and uniforms changed. Royal blue became powder blue, the unpretentious block lettering with the *V* made to look like a hoop replaced by a chic, futuristic font. And the players donning the unis were just as unrecognizable. Ehlo and Price were traded. Nance as well as veteran all-star center Brad Daugherty sustained career-ending injuries. Before long the team became bottom-feeding, a revolving door of recent college-phenom guards destined never to fulfill their promise, onetime all-star forwards well past their prime, and slow, white big men typically of Eastern European descent.

I must've caught the Cavs close to fifty times at the Coliseum. I saw three, maybe four games at the Gund. And yet it was more than the move and accompanying ineptitude that led me to lose interest.

Basketball was the first organized sport I ever played, starting in fourth grade, on one of our church's Catholic Youth Organization teams. I continued to play through junior varsity sophomore year of high school, and was both good and serious enough by the summer before tenth grade to spend a week in Pittsburgh at Five Star, the renowned camp where Jordan and dozens of other NBA stars had first caught the attention of scouts and recruiters. Then I stopped growing. Nobody hustled or sacrificed his body more. My knees and elbows were always strawberried from diving after loose balls and taking charges. After breaking my nose in a sled-riding accident halfway through freshman season, I finished it out wearing a ridiculous plastic face mask. But despite my willingness to mix it up, at five foot eleven I wasn't much of a presence underneath and wasn't a good enough ball handler or shooter to play the perimeter. The game was losing its fun. The JV practiced with the varsity and, as many suicides and laps as we ran, we might as well have been the cross-country team. Also, the varsity coach was a Bobby Knight type and the prospect of spending the next two years being berated and projectile spat on wasn't exactly appealing.

Then there was the divorce. I don't know how much it had to do with me souring on the game, but I suppose the fact that it coincided with that last season in Richfield can't be overlooked.

Mom pulled for the Cavs as hard as anyone and loved going to the Coliseum. And, of course, there was Grandpa's connection to the game. However, baseball was always more her sport. Basketball was Dad's.

Goodyear had its own gym, left over from the years of the industrial-league teams, and every day at lunch Dad and some coworkers would play pickup. He also played in a night league. When it came to personal expenditures, neither of my parents was extravagant—couldn't afford to be after spoiling me so—but the one thing Dad splurged on was high-tops. He owned the first Reebok Pumps, the first Larry Johnson Converse, the first Air Jordans. (He had just as much antipathy for MJ as myself or anyone else within a hundred-mile radius, but those shoes were so sweet neither of us cared that it constituted a betrayal.)

When the weather was nice, as soon as he got home from work he'd change out of his suit and join me in the driveway for scuttle— what one-on-one went by when he was my age, he claimed, though to this day he's the only one I've ever heard use the term. Even when the weather *wasn't* nice—plenty of times we'd be out there in the dead of winter missing wildly thanks to our gloves. *Competitive* wouldn't begin to describe those games—more like *knock-down, drag-out*. Often, scrambling for a rebound or going for a steal, one of us would wind up yowling in pain after our momentum had carried us into the thick stand of sharp-needled pines lining the drive. Eventually it would be paved in concrete, but for years the drive was brittle asphalt, easy to slip and fall and scrape your hands and knees on.

Dad had a hair-trigger jump shot and was equally quick with the dribble—play too close and he'd blow right by. Usually by the time we were through I'd be so incensed I'd wing the ball at him and run into the house crying. Mom was always imploring him to take it easy on me, and sometimes he would, but then I'd refuse to play. If I was going to beat him, I wanted it to be fair and square.

It wasn't till seventh grade that I finally won a game. I can't remember the particulars, how close the score was or the shot I hit to ice it, but I do recall it feeling not as sweet as I thought it would. Perhaps I saw it as marking a turning point in our relationship, a sort of passing of the torch, my entrée into manhood, and was a little sad to see things change. I didn't think too much about it, though, as he continued to whip my butt 90 percent of the time; were we to lace it up right now I'd put the odds at even money.

If any event marked a turning point, needless to say, it was the night he left. Basketball played a part in that, too. After he and Mom sat me down on the couch and explained, after I watched from my bedroom window as he packed up his car and drove off, I was so numb and confused and desperate for something to do, anything to take my mind off, I grabbed the shredded-up Spalding and started dribbling around the block. Close to two hours I kept at it, just dribbling, around and around and around.

From then on a basketball was my madeleine. Every time I laid hands on one, my subconscious was delivered back to that night until at last it bucked. Maybe that's why I quit playing. Or maybe— though my love for and idolization of him never would've allowed me to admit such a thing—I was furious at Dad for leaving, and, knowing how much he loved the game, gave it up to punish him. Maybe the coach was just too much of an asshole. Or maybe I wasn't good enough.

Same with the Cavs. Could be I equated their bailing on Richfield with Dad's going and hated them for it—for upending my world more than it'd already been. Could be even if they'd stayed put I'd have stopped following them due to the pain of remembering all the times the three of us spent at the Coliseum together. Or could be they just started to suck and the tickets were overpriced and the seats shitty and the drive to Cleveland a pain in the ass. Whatever the case, not only was that first year of the Gund my last playing, it was my last as any semblance of a Cavs fan—as a basketball fan, period.

I guess it would've had to be junior year of college, that night Sully called up near breathless with excitement. He'd just watched our alma mater, Walsh Jesuit, get obliterated by its archrival, St. Vincent–St. Mary, by twenty-something points, or roughly the total scored by some St. V freshman variously described by my besotted best friend as "a man child," "a man among boys," "a freak," "a machine," "a stud," "a monster," and "Superman." "LeBron James," Sully said. "Don't forget that name."

Not likely. Soon I couldn't talk to Mom or Dad or Claire or any of the family back home—St. V alumni all—without their mentioning the kid: how he landed the cover of *Sports Illustrated;* how he unsuccessfully petitioned the NBA to enter the draft after his junior year; how his mom bought him a Hummer; how he accidentally backed that Hummer into some eighty-year-old woman's car; how he got suspended a couple games for accepting merchandise gratis from a Cleveland clothing store; how demand to see him play had so ballooned that the games were moved to U of A's ten-thousand-seat arena and even then people were being turned away. (To have caught him, as had Sully, at that dank cubbyhole on the corner of Maple and Market streets became akin to seeing the Beatles at the Cavern Club or Bruce Springsteen at the Stone Pony.)

As dramatic as things were off the court, LeBron's dominance on it became almost humdrum for its regularity. His freshman year, he led St. V to a state championship. As a sophomore he did so again, in the process garnering Ohio's "Mr. Basketball" award recognizing the top player in the state. He received the honor a second time his junior year, and an unprecedented third as a senior after guiding the Irish to their third state title in four seasons. In its near hundred-year history, the school had won state in boys' hoops just twice before.

Such otherworldly talent, and homegrown at that . . . you'd think the Cavs selecting LeBron with the first pick of the 2003 draft—as well as their corresponding decision to ditch the powder-blue palette for the wine and gold of the franchise's infancy—would've been just the thing to resurrect my interest in the team, the game. On the contrary, it repelled me even further.

It wasn't his forgoing college. The way I saw it, any teenager who'd opt for the grueling, road-wearying life of the NBA over four years of ghostwritten term papers, booster-club fetes, and nubile, eager-to-please coeds was to be commended, not condemned. Nor was it simple envy, me wishing those signs erected around the city limits welcomed visitors to *my* hometown instead of his, me lusting to be considered Akron's native son. Had I felt so possessive of the place, I wouldn't have split the first chance I got. It wasn't even his wearing number 23 in homage to Jordan. Five years my junior, he'd probably never even heard of the Coliseum. All he knew were the Gund Arena, perennial cellar-dwelling Cavs. Who was he supposed to have idolized? Bobby Sura?

It was the money I took issue with. Before draft day he had inked a seven-year endorsement deal with Nike worth $90 million as well as a $1 million, five-year contract with Upper Deck trading cards that came with an additional $1 million signing bonus. As the first overall pick, he was entitled by the league's rookie pay scale to more than $12 million over four years. Seventeen years old, not a minute logged as a pro, and already guaranteed in excess of $100 million.

Nobody deserved that—except maybe cancer doctors and heart surgeons. What I had no way of knowing at the time was that when it ultimately came to Mom's fight for survival, LeBron James would prove just as instrumental and so deserving of every penny.

III.

She spent the first couple months of the basketball season in one of the two glassed-in rooms in the G-53 cardiothoracic ICU battling recurring pneumonia and infection, comatose most of the time, either from low blood pressure or sedation, which was used along with wrist restraints for when she'd come to and be so disoriented she'd start yanking at her trach and IVs and try getting out of bed. Still, I'd turn the TV to the Cavs whenever they were on, figuring perhaps the squeak of sneakers and the organ playing "Charge" might seep through and loose some memory of a better time. The turnaround jumper I hit in overtime of the fourth-grade CYO championship to help upset undefeated St. Francis Xavier and get my name in the *Beacon-Journal*. Or the time Dad got Cavs tickets through work and we got all the way to the Coliseum's turnstiles only to discover he'd mixed up the date and they were for the following week. Had it just been the three of us, we'd have gone back home, but I'd brought a friend and Dad didn't want to embarrass me. The only tickets still left that close to tip-off were eighth row, center court: a hundred dollars each. After that, whenever we'd go to a game, Mom would razz him about remembering to check the tickets.

As much as I'd heard about LeBron, I'd seen little of him besides the occasional *SportsCenter* highlight. It wasn't until after a month or so of watching him all four quarters, night in and night out, that I finally believed the hype. He could do it all—one game leading the team in rebounds, the next in assists, the next in steals, sometimes in all three, and almost always in points. What most impressed me, though, was his temperament. It was impossible to believe he was just twenty-two. So poised, so composed, never too high or too low, never taking things too seriously or not seriously enough, the epitome of even keel. This was something I'd been striving for myself—to not get too excited when Mom had a good day or too down when things stalled or backslid.

Between this and our shared heritage—from Akron; an only child; an obvious bond with his mom, herself a single parent, always courtside cheering him on—I found much to relate to and root for in LeBron, though still not as much as I would in another Cavalier, improbably enough a seven-foot-four, bald-headed Lithuanian.

Zydrunas Ilgauskas. One of those lumbering, pasty-faced, ESL behemoths the Cavs always played at center following Brad Daugherty's retirement. Except whereas the rest had languished in Cleveland only a year or two before moving on to less polluted and subarctic pastures, Z had been mired there since 1996—chronic foot injuries confining him to the bench the majority of his first six seasons and rendering him untradable. However, things had been looking up in the new millennium. He'd twice been named an all-star and the previous season helped the Cavs make the playoffs for the first time in seven years. With the current season more than half gone, they looked assured of heading back, thanks in no small part to Z, who'd lately become the franchise's all-time leader in offensive rebounds.

Then in early February, with Mom amid her fifth month in the hospital, his wife was hospitalized after prematurely going into labor. On Valentine's Day of all days, she delivered stillborn twins, a boy and a girl, what would've been the couple's first children.

Sport is no stranger to personal tragedy: a heart attack in the midst of play, a drug overdose, an incurable illness, a plane crash. Just that past October from Mom's room I'd watched live CNN footage of the smoldering Upper East Side high-rise where New York Yankees pitcher and novice pilot Cory Lidle met his end. I was scarcely moved by the news. Such was the life of a world-class athlete: befallen by only the most sensational of calamities. What happened to Ilgauskas and his wife, on the other hand—a miscarriage, a misfortune likely experienced by hundreds if not thousands of families that very same day—was a misery prevalent like our own. The very mundanity made it heartrending, him empathetic.

That and his unwillingness—or sheer inability—to conceal his grief. He'd always borne a passing resemblance to an extra in a zombie movie; when he rejoined the team two weeks later he looked ready to play the undead lead. His eyes were sunken, sleepless, his skin more pallid than ever, translucent practically, as if it'd been days since he was last outside, since his shades at home weren't drawn. He hung his head a little longer retreating on defense after a missed free throw, yanked off his warm-ups a little less forcefully on his way to the scorer's table. On the bench he'd often appear lost in thought, staring at the near court despite play having headed back the other way.

True, his statistics seemed to suggest he was holding up fine; he averaged roughly the same points and rebounds per game after the miscarriage as he had before. But as we'd learned with Mom and weaning, numbers were rarely a reliable indicator of how one was feeling.

His productivity made no difference to me anyhow. For all I cared, he could've gone scoreless every night. What mattered, what I took inspiration from, was that he was on the court at all, that he was simply getting out of bed each morning.

I could go on. About how spending so many months in Cleveland, becoming familiar with the city to an extent I'd never been, made me as proprietary of the team as when they were in Richfield. How the game's often frantic pace, as well as its preoccupation with timekeeping—the game and shot clocks; the three-, five-, and ten-second rules; the full and twenty-second time-outs—meshed perfectly with weaning's anxious, clock-watching mentality. How all the days Mom, Dad, and I spent together, plus the constancy and tenderness he showed her, made it sometimes seem as if he'd never left. But mostly my reawakening as a Cavs backer was out of necessity. Weeks, months at a time in the same small room with nothing but the date on the assignment board and the appearance of the weekend-only nurses to differentiate one day from the next, I had to give myself something to get excited about, to look forward to.

We watched the Indians and the Browns as well as *American Idol* and *Survivor, Dancing with the Stars* and *The Amazing Race, Deal or*

No Deal, The Biggest Loser, The Apprentice, Project Runway with the same fervency, for the same reason. (Not *Top Chef* or *Hell's Kitchen*—the sight of all that food was too cruel.) But the regularity of the baseball schedule soon made it as monotonous as everything else—until the playoffs, anyway—while football and reality game shows coming just once a week underscored how much time was passing and how swiftly and how little progress was being made. With a game every two, three days, basketball was the ideal diversion.

For us, therefore, a lot more was riding on the Cavs' playoff success than bragging rights or decades' worth of redemption. Every game, every series won ensured at least a few more days of anticipation, a few more treasured opportunities for escape. In one of those uncanny confluences that seemed to punctuate the entire ordeal, not only did the G-and-J-tube procedure fall on the same date Mom turned fifty-nine; that night was game five of the Eastern Conference Finals versus the top-seeded and heavily favored Detroit Pistons. And given the outcome of the procedure, the need for distraction was greater than ever.

The G-tube was placed with no trouble. The J-tube, however, proved too tricky; as the doctor who performed the procedure explained, maneuvering the endoscope that far into the small intestine was tantamount to slipping a straw back in its wrapper by handling just the straw. And there was more. While passing the endoscope through the esophagus, they'd discovered a strange-looking lesion. Most likely it was scar tissue from all the intubating and extubating, but a biopsy had been taken just to be sure.

It was the second biopsy in three days. Mom didn't know about either of them. Until the results were back, the doctor on rotation saw no use in discouraging or scaring her any more than she already was. But *I* knew, and herein lay my central dilemma, in this instance as well as with respect to the whole damn mess. Be it a bad dream, a bad breakup, an impending term paper or article deadline, or the feared contraction of a sexually transmitted disease, whenever the least bit worried or afraid, I'd always scurried to Mom for reassurance and guidance—a dependence more pronounced because of the divorce and being an only child. Now, more terrified than ever, I couldn't. Not really. Sure, there were those times I allowed myself to crack, when I'd scoot the high-backed chair as close to the bed as it'd go and lay my head on the mattress edge or on her distended stomach even and let her stroke my ever-lengthening hair. But, with a couple exceptions, that's exactly what I was doing—*allowing, letting;* those times were intentional, not involuntary, meant to help her as much as myself, remind her of the fact she wasn't just some sick person stuck in a hospital, that she was a mother, *my* mother, that she had a purpose, that she was still needed.

Because she was—God, was she ever. Her mere presence, the fact that she was simply still alive, was a comfort exceeding words. But when it came to instilling confidence and deflecting fear, our roles had unquestionably reversed.

So that when I first got a look at the G-tube—the incision site caked with dried blood and oozing pus, the tube affixed to a catheter bag by a length of durable plastic tubing no different from the kind I'd picked up at Home Depot senior year of high school to make a beer bong—I had to resist crying. And when Mom began to cry herself from frustration over the omission of the J-tube, I made sure to stress the positive, how the G-tube would help the nausea and vomiting. This seemed to pacify her for the little while she was awake. The lingering effects of the anesthesia kept her dozing throughout the afternoon and evening. I thought about waking her up for tip-off but let her rest instead.

So far the Cavs-Pistons series couldn't have been more nip and tuck. The total combined point margin of the first four games, split by the home teams, was just fourteen, with the widest single margin being six points in game three. Game five would be closer yet—the score tied to begin the fourth quarter and neither team extending more than a three-point lead until halfway through, when Detroit ran off ten unanswered points. Up seven with just over three minutes to go and the capacity Palace of Auburn Hills crowd in full throat, the Pistons were in complete control.

Then LeBron started heating up.

A layup to stunt Detroit's momentum and get the Cavs back on the board. After a teammate split a pair of free throws, a three from the top of the key to cut the deficit to one. With just thirty seconds left, a thunderous dunk to regain the lead. Detroit's all-star guard Chauncey Billups immediately answered with a three to put the Pistons back up two, but on the next Cavs possession LeBron slashed to the hoop for *another* dunk to tie the score, give himself thirty points on the night, and send the game to overtime.

During the commercial break, a few people rushed past Mom's room—other patients' loved ones hurrying to make it to their cars and Joe Tait's play-by-play. Others not so daring headed for the bathroom or the ice machine or just a quick walk to stretch their legs.

Such a flurry of activity for that time of night was unusual. Normally I'd be the only family member left, the floor silent but for the trilling of vent alarms. I worried the commotion might disturb her, but she stayed out cold.

So far, the only time she'd awoken, and that briefly, was when Nick administered her nine o'clock meds. Aside from popping in once in a while to check the score—and thereupon giving the thumbs-up or a sullen shake of the head—he left us in peace. By the start of OT he and the rest of the nurses, RTs—both those newly arrived for the midnight shift and those they were replacing—and even the mild-mannered Latino custodian whose sole responsibility, it seemed, was to nightly mop and wax reSCU's thirty-odd-foot stretch of linoleum, gave up any pretense of working and ensconced themselves throughout the rooms.

LeBron picked up where he'd left off in regulation, scoring all nine of Cleveland's points, including another timely slam off a nifty backdoor pass from Z. Detroit stayed tough, however, and forced the game to a second extra period. That's when LeBron flat-out caught fire—when, as history will undoubtedly judge, he joined the ranks of the NBA's all-time elite.

A step-back from the wing. Good. Forty-one points. Behind-the-back dribble to shake Billups into a top-of-the-key jumper. Good again. Forty-three. Falling-away three with two defenders in his face. Got it. Forty-six. Still, the Pistons would not wilt. Eleven seconds left. All square at 107. Cavs' ball out of a time-out.

The sideline inbounds goes to LeBron just shy of half-court. The rest of the team vacates the lane. He waits. *Ten. Nine.* Billups, arms out and knees bent in textbook defensive stance, encroaches. Still he waits. *Eight. Seven.* Billups closes, shading LeBron to his left, his weaker hand. *Six. Five.* He goes. No hesitation, no tentativeness. Across the three-point arc, a couple steps past the free-throw line, where, with Billups right on his hip, he's greeted by the rest of the Pistons, all four of them. A Cavalier teammate stands in one corner uncovered. LeBron doesn't even pretend to look, nor does the teammate pretend to expect a pass. LeBron rises. So do the Pistons, one and all. When they land, however, he's still in the air, scooping the ball from down by his ankles and spinning it right-handed off the glass, outside the target square, with an exact dollop of English.

Cavs lead 109–107. Two point two seconds to go.

If I said the G Building shook, naturally you wouldn't believe it. I'm not even sure I do. Yet when you figure the hundreds of patients and all their families and friends held captive by the drama plus the enormity of staff, everyone jumping up and down in unison, it's not so outside the realm of possibility. I wasn't exempt. So far, out of consideration for Mom, I'd remained reserved—at most giving tiny fist pumps or swearing under my breath. But when that shot went down, my self-control finally failed me. I too leapt from the chair and added my shouts to those emanating from what by the sound of it was every room on the floor—the din louder still as Billups's desperation jumper rattled out and the final horn blared.

With it, I turned from the TV to apologize for my outburst. I'd indeed roused her, but her eyelids were again growing heavy.

"We did it," I said. "We won."

Mom smiled and mouthed, "Yay," then drifted back off.

All told, LeBron played fifty-one of fifty-eight minutes and scored forty-eight points, including Cleveland's last twenty-five. Two nights later he missed a triple-double by two assists and the Cavs won handily. At game's end, before his head coach or even his mom, the first person LeBron rushed to embrace was Z; leaping into his arms, he elicited the first smile I'd seen from the giant in months. Mom stayed awake the entire game—all the anesthesia in the world couldn't have kept her from sharing in this moment almost forty years in the making—and we too hugged—again, as best we could.

On the drive home I passed an impromptu block party that'd broken out at the East Fifty-fifth and Woodland gas station. Subwoofers filling the air with discordant bass lines. Thirty, forty people drinking and dancing—some on car roofs. Southbound on 77, a bedsheet spray-painted THANKQ LEBRON had already been strung from an overpass. For miles drivers in both directions laid on their horns, myself included. For the first time ever, the Cavs were going to the NBA Finals—*the Cleveland Cavaliers!* It was the happiest and most hopeful I'd felt in months.

It wouldn't last long. The next day the results from the first biopsy came back. The tumor in her lung was undiminished. A PET scan a few days later would reveal the cancer had spread to a nearby lymph node. In the Finals, the Cavs would get swept by San Antonio.

CHAPTER TWO

I.

Usually we only talked Sundays, but on my way downtown to the catering-company headquarters that Thursday afternoon, having caught both the N and the 1 trains just as I'd reached their platforms, I had some time to kill. Given the odds of such an expeditious commute, I should've made for the OTB at Church and Broadway, but instead I got out at Franklin, walked over to the little park at Duane and Hudson, took a seat on one of the benches, and, after a couple minutes basking in the balmy, more early-June than late-September weather, decided to give her a call.

She must've known it was me from the caller ID but still sounded surprised, even more so when I told her I wasn't calling except to say hi—surprised and happy, thrilled really. We talked about how her day was going, the party I was working. I was turning twenty-seven Monday. She asked what Elaine and I had planned. I told her we were going to dinner.

"Go get yourself a decent shirt and pair of pants," she said. "My treat."

She'd been on me about how I dressed since sophomore year at

Walsh. It was a college-preparatory school. Collared shirts and dress pants were mandatory. That'd been part of my reason for going there. Having spent the mid-eighties through the early nineties in public school, where popularity demanded subjecting oneself to such ridiculous trends as Hypercolor and those atrocious, pajama-bottom-looking Skidz, I relished the chance to throw on any old polo shirt and wear the same khakis three days in a row. Yet Walsh turned out to be even more of a fashion show: all the mallet-wielding men on horseback and drawn spinnakers, the signal flags and alligators. I tried to keep up my first year—at my lowest, bought a pair of brown suede saddle shoes—then revolted. Grew my hair long. Began shopping at thrift stores. The dress code merely stipulated collars and pockets without rivets, so I started channeling John Travolta in *Saturday Night Fever*—butterfly collars, bell-bottoms. Mom couldn't stand it.

"Nobody's gonna take you seriously in those things," she'd say.

"Fine by me," I'd say. "If they're that superficial, I don't wanna associate with 'em anyway."

"All that money we're paying, and you show up there looking like that."

"I'd think you'd be glad, then, much as I'm saving you."

"In that case, I should've had your dad hang on to his old clothes—I'd have saved even more."

Badgering not doing the trick, she tried a more subtle tack. One Christmas she handed me a J. Crew catalog and pen and told me to pick out what I wanted. I gave it back with the girls in the intimates section circled. Then she joined me in the thrift store, skimming the racks alongside me searching for the least off-putting paisleys and plaids. She could've grounded me, but I was a good kid, a two-sport athlete with a B-plus average who generally kept out of trouble. She probably figured I was entitled to a little rebelliousness, and if passé haberdashery was my outlet rather than standing kegs or sparking bowls or bashing mailboxes or prematurely divesting virginity, she should count herself lucky. Plus I think there was part of her that was proud of my individualist streak. I know there was.

One night senior year a ceremony was held in the gym to recognize us National Honor Society students. She'd grown more tolerant of my wardrobe the last few semesters, largely because I'd branched into booze and vandalism—still not sex, thanks to her job as a public-health nurse—and she had bigger worries. (A predawn fiasco involving a friend's parents' van, a neighbor's portable basketball hoop, and a foot chase with two infuriatingly in-shape patrolmen springs most readily to mind.) Even so, no way on such an honorific occasion would she have let me out of the house in my favorite chocolate-brown JCPenney's three-piece. So I didn't even bother: just put on a white shirt and my lone tie that wasn't a kipper and some navy Dockers. Still, I couldn't resist adding my own stamp. I loved hip-hop, and outside of class when I wore jeans would sport a sag. That night when my name was called and I proceeded up the aisle to receive my pin, my waistband was around my knees.

"Your mother nearly got in a fistfight," Dad said on the ride home.

As I was walking up, another mother sitting nearby had sneered to her husband, "I feel sorry for his parents."

"We're his parents," Mom shot back. "What of it?"

The other mother tried to laugh it off, but Mom stared her down until the woman grew so uncomfortable she and her husband got up and moved. In the car, Mom was still irate—"Embarrassed for me? *I'm* embarrassed for *her*!"—but not once, then nor ever, did she blame me. Exasperated as she so often was by my attire, she was never ashamed.

Things got a bit better when I went off to Florida and, due to the heat, ditched the polyester and eventually chopped my hair. They got better still when after college I moved to New York and discovered, absent the proximate convenience of dorm life, hooking up was no longer as easy as a twelve of Icehouse and D'Angelo's *Voodoo*. That first you had to go on these things called dates, usually involving a dinner, expectantly at restaurants whose menus didn't include ninety-nine-cent options and whose requisites for service were thereby a bit more extensive than just a shirt and shoes. By the time I met Elaine, I was wearing a belt and using an iron and everything. Naturally, Mom was elated. But she was still my mom.

"You should be getting your package tomorrow or Saturday," she said that afternoon. Every birthday since college she'd sent me a confetti-filled box containing my favorite Acme walnut brownies, a copy of *The New Yorker* indicating the renewal of my subscription, and a fifty-dollar check. "Just use the check I sent and let me know the difference and I'll cut you another one."

"I'm good," I said—still her son, after all.

"All right. Tell Elaine I tried."

My birthday dinner scheduled for Sunday night, we got off the phone promising to talk Monday.

"Five thirty-eight," she said. "The minute you came into this world."

Work that night went past midnight. I didn't get to bed till three or so. When I finally woke up, a little after eleven, I had a voicemail from Dad asking me to call him. I didn't talk to him except Sundays, either, but could tell by the urgency and poorly concealed plaintiveness in his voice he wasn't just calling to say hi. I went into the second bedroom, which I'd turned into an office upon moving in with Elaine nearly a year earlier, took a seat at my desk, and called him back.

"Your mom collapsed at work," he said. "They took her by ambulance to Akron General. That's all I know. Claire called and told me. Melanie called her. I'm just dropping off the work van and heading over. Claire was on her way when she called. Melanie rode in the ambulance. Call Claire."

I did. As it was relayed to her by Melanie—Mom's coworker and best friend for almost a decade—Mom had been complaining of shortness of breath all morning. Melanie kept wanting to drive her to the emergency room but Mom wouldn't let her. Finally, when it got so bad Mom no longer had the strength to stand, Melanie called 911.

"They think she had a heart attack in the ambulance," Claire said. "They're in right now doing a catheterization. We haven't talked to the doctor yet. It's just Melanie and me right now. Roger and Alice and your dad are on their way. You better come home, Sean. It's serious."

Of course, any heart attack is serious. But Claire wasn't being naïve. Her husband, my uncle Max, had his first major heart attack when he was just thirty-seven. Then came another minor one a few months later. Then triple-bypass surgery. Ten years later a double. Then, ten years after that, one finally got him for good. No, when it came to heart attacks, Claire was like a native Californian with earthquakes, able at the very first rumble to distinguish a 2.3 from a

7.6. For *her* to say it was serious meant you damn sure better believe it was.

After hanging up with Claire, I sat there a minute and wept. Mom had sounded fine on the phone the day before, better than fine. What had I missed? Had I sensed deep down something was wrong? Was that why I'd called—some filial telepathy? What if I hadn't? At least if she died I'd got to speak to her one last time.

I rolled the chair over to the window so I could look down on Mr. Angeletti's garden. It contained every kind of herb imaginable, plus all sorts of flowers, a grape arbor fashioned out of broom handles and sprouting leaves the size of catcher's mitts, even a tall, potted cactus. Looking at it always relaxed me.

The owner of the three-floor row house, Mr. Angeletti was in his late eighties with a significant hunch and a full head of white hair. He and his wife had lived there something like sixty years. They'd come over from Italy. Neither of them spoke much English. They raised three kids there. One, now in her fifties and suffering from some developmental disability, still lived with Mr. Angeletti on the first and second floors.

Just after New Year's Mrs. Angeletti had passed. No one had told us. We'd heard she was in the hospital. Then one night we came home to find a bunch of people clad in black crowding the entrance-way and eating off plastic plates.

A couple weeks later, I was leaving the house for work just as Mr. Angeletti was coming out of the laundry room by the front door. It was the first time I'd seen him since. I told him how sorry I was. He began to cry.

"She gone," he kept saying, over and over, five or six times.

I wasn't sure what to do, so I just put my hand on his shoulder.

Now, as I was crying, looking down into the garden, he came shuffling outside. He always wore the same black short-sleeved button-down, gray slacks, and black shoes. He went over to the small shed and took up the broom leaning there and began sweeping the patio. It was the last time I ever saw him. He died a few months later.

I called the airline and booked my ticket. Then I called Elaine at work.

"Do you want me to come?" she asked.

Not only would she be a huge comfort, Elaine also had one of the sharpest memories of anyone I'd ever met. Usually this was a source of aggrievement—on anniversaries, in particular—but not now, foreseeing as I did myself and the rest of the family being too distraught to retain everything, *anything* the doctors said.

Not to say Elaine wouldn't be distraught herself. She and Mom had hit it off from the first time they'd met, and in the year and a half since had grown close. Sundays, after we'd caught up, she'd ask me to put Elaine on the phone. Lately they'd started swapping recipes over e-mail. As far as Mom was concerned, Elaine was family. In which case, who was I to say whether she could or couldn't go? She had as much right to be there as anyone.

Most of all, having her around would help keep me from breaking down. So long as Mom was alive and there were options to be weighed, decisions to be made, I had to maintain my composure. And like any guy, I'd be less prone to lose it front of my girl.

A part of me, though, didn't want her there. As an only child, I'd always been selfish in everything, turmoil being no exception. Along those same lines was another reason, one I wasn't conscious of at the time and that even now remains fairly murky, difficult to explain without sounding Oedipal or just plain creepy. In addition to having son feelings for my mother, as a result of the divorce, as well as my hormonally fraught age when it occurred, and also of my being an only child, a *male* child, I had what might be construed as husband feelings, too. From all the meals we'd eaten as just the two of us, the household chores we'd shared, the uncensored nature of our confidence, I felt a loyalty and dutifulness more befitting of spouse than spawn. The part of me that didn't want Elaine there was worried that Mom, when she needed me most, might feel she was being cast aside. Again.

I told Elaine I'd think about it while I packed. Not sure how long I'd be gone or if I'd have time to check a bag at LaGuardia—and even if I did, not wanting to waste time at Akron-Canton Airport waiting around baggage claim—I threw a pair of pants and five days' worth of shirts, socks, and underwear into a carry-on; took a quick shower and dressed; and, after finishing with them, packed contact-lens solution, toothbrush, and the rest of my toiletries. I also packed a book. I remember thinking that was weird even as I was doing it, knowing that no way could I concentrate enough to read. But I threw it in anyway, not quite ready to accept that this would be no usual plane trip.

Then I called Elaine back.

"I want you to come," I said.

"Already booked my ticket," she said.

I never loved her more.

II.

I called Dad to let him know we'd get to the hospital around five. He offered to pick us up, but I insisted he stay there in case he was needed. Really, I just wasn't comfortable with him driving all worked up. I wasn't comfortable driving myself. Elaine could've, but it made no sense spending a couple hundred bucks a day for a rental car when there'd be Mom's Corolla. So I called Sully.

Opposite as we were, I still don't know how we got to be best friends. He had four brothers. I was an only child. He listened to Dave Matthews. I preferred Cleveland's very own Bone Thugs-N-Harmony. (Devo was formed in Akron? The Pretenders' Chrissie Hynde went to public Firestone High? I could have cared less growing up. But, oh, the swell of pride whenever I'd hear "1st of Tha Month" or "Tha Crossroads.") Sully was borderline ADD, never studied, got terrible grades. He was on the golf team. I despised golf. Of all of Walsh's label whores, he might've been the biggest—wore Brooks Brothers shirts with silver cuff links and Johnston & Murphy wing tips he shined every few days. To pay for his habit, he worked landscaping seventy hours a week in the summer. Summers I played baseball. I drank. He never touched the stuff.

About the only thing we did have in common was our devotion to our mothers. His taught math at Walsh, and though you'd think he'd have been embarrassed always having her around, pretended she wasn't there, he was instead constantly dropping by her class to say hi and see how she was—and to boost me. First semester senior year I had Mrs. Sully for pre-calculus. Sully had study hall that period. A couple times a month he'd come in just as class was starting and tell her we had some urgent student-council business.

"Can't wait, Mom. Needed to be taken care of like twenty minutes ago."

Knowing he was full of it, Mrs. Sully would cut me anyway and we'd go play Ping-Pong.

The reason Walsh had a Ping-Pong table was because I wanted to go somewhere warm for college. Worried I didn't have enough extracurriculars to get in anywhere out of state, I decided near the end of junior year to run for student-council president and asked Sully to be my VP. His three older brothers had also gone to Walsh, and his younger brother was a sophomore. His aunt taught there, too. Around school, his surname might as well have been Kennedy. We were a shoo-in.

Just to be safe, having learned a thing or two from all Dad's years in advertising, I launched a full-on marketing blitz, papering the halls and lockers and stairwells with posters and flyers. Other candidates' read VOTE 4 MOLLY AND MEREDITH or KARL DIETZ FOR PREZ. Ours were more original. The flyer I remember best was a picture I'd found in *People* of Puck from MTV's *The Real World*. He was at a party with a drink in his hand and an arm around some girl. I cut her head out and pasted in my most recent yearbook photo. HE KNOWS PUCK went the slogan.

If that still didn't cinch things, there was our stump speech. One day each of the three lunch periods crowded into the theater to hear the candidates lay out their agendas. The others' included blood drives, more salt on the front walkway in winter, increased wheelchair accessibility. Sully and I vowed a Snapple machine in the caf, an underwear-only theme dance, and the conversion of a storage room into a Ping-Pong room. We got a standing ovation all three times.

Ping-Pong was the only promise we'd make good on, and even

that didn't last the whole year. Kids started bringing in their own paddles, some costing as much as a hundred dollars and carried in leather over-the-shoulder bags. Betting grew rampant. More than once faculty had to break up some shoving match resulting from a disputed out call. Some of the teachers themselves got caught up. One, a lay theology instructor, would give his classes study hall and then go play. He was heavyset, and one day when lunging for a ball lost his balance and put his ass through the wall. The table was removed soon after.

Of course, my transcripts didn't mention what a farce our time in office had been, and from the small, private University of Tampa I received a "Presidential Scholarship," awarded to students having displayed exceptional leadership skills. It covered half my tuition each year. Sully never quit bitching about it.

"Let me get this straight—I get you elected and you get paid to go lie in the sun?"

He went to U of A, part-time, all he could afford from landscaping and busing tables at Luigi's, an Italian restaurant downtown, during the winter. To further cut down on expenses, he continued living at home.

Mom loved Sully. Since he didn't drink, he was often the designated driver, and, unlike the rest of the guys, who'd just honk when picking me up, he always came inside to chat with her. Until they got onto the subject of politics. Then chatting turned to ranting—Mom a dyed-in-the-wool Democrat, Sully incapable of being more of a Republican if he'd had tusks. Party affiliations aside, she always said he should run for mayor—passionate, outgoing, and handsome as he was. After I left for Florida, he'd still drop by the house every now and then—to gloat over the Lewinsky and pardons scandals, but also to talk about school with Mom. Having graduated from U of A's nursing school less than a decade before, she'd had a few of the same classes, same professors even. Also they both had all those siblings—I'm sure that had something to do with their kinship.

For Sully and Dad, the linchpin was golf. Dad was even better at it than at basketball—scratch throughout much of his forties. He'd long tried to foster in me a love of the game. I did my best to oblige. We'd go hit a bucket of balls or play the par-three at the complex across the street from his apartment, but after my third eight in a row or yet *another* wormburner, clubs and expletives would go flying. How could I hit an eighty-mile-an-hour curve three hundred feet yet completely whiff on that tiny little ball standing still? It infuriated me. I wanted no part. And so when it came to that infernal sport, Sully was Dad's surrogate son. A heel injury kept him off the team the last two years at Walsh, but he could still score in the mid-seventies. One of his brothers was assistant superintendent at Firestone Country Club—site of the PGA's Bridgestone Invitational, née NEC Invitational, née World Series of Golf—and Sully would get himself and Dad on the prestigious South Course at least once a summer.

Both Mom and Dad were there at Sully's commencement. Five and a half years it took him. An uncle was a bigwig at some insurance company and got him a position with their Chicago office. He was making great money, living a block from Lake Michigan in a doorman building with a rooftop pool. A year later he was back home with his parents. The job was too sedentary. He couldn't stand being cooped up in a cubicle all day. He still didn't drink, and it was hard meeting people without going to the bars. He missed his family.

Most of the guys were surprised when he decided to become a

cop. Not me. The precision of the uniform, every hour of every work-day holding something different. Mom was concerned for his safety and hated guns—made him leave his in the car whenever he stopped by—yet it also meshed with her hopes for him. "Now he'll *definitely* be able to beat out the Don," she'd say, referring to then-three-term Mayor Plusquellic, so nicknamed not only because that was his name—Donald—but because his stranglehold on the office, despite continual upticks in unemployment and crime, was starting to feel tantamount to a mob boss's tenure.

Sully was a couple hours from the end of his shift when I'd called, and met Elaine and me at the airport in uniform. I'd seen him in it before but never could get over how different it made him look. He was so brimming with confidence and stood up so straight it was as if he'd gained six inches—and, from the protective padding beneath his shirt, put on twenty pounds. It wasn't all padding. The academy had filled him out well. And his shaved head only upped his impos-ingness. The Glock on his hip didn't hurt, either.

We didn't waste time with pleasantries. He simply grabbed my shoulder and squeezed, then took Elaine's bag and led us to the parking lot. I was hoping for the cruiser—he could flash the lights and do ninety—but he'd brought his little red sedan. It didn't matter. He still did ninety.

III.

Dad was waiting outside. Unlike Sully, he didn't dispense with the small talk but was instead quite garrulous as he led us through the lobby, past the visitors' library and chapel, the tiny gift shop and even smaller cafeteria, the oncoming wave of administrative personnel heading home. He asked about the flight, commented on how long Elaine's hair had got since she'd come back with me at Christmas, and, as we waited for the elevator, peered closely at Sully's badge and made some crack about supermarket toy machines.

Partly this was his usual outgoingness; partly I suspected—for I felt it, too—relief that she'd survived the catheterization. But largely, I figured, he was feigning this lightheartedness to shield me as long as possible from the imminent pain of seeing Mom the way she was. At least until we were in the elevator and he told us what happened to cousin Jeff, the husband of Claire's daughter, Andrea. Then his amusement was entirely in earnest.

"There we all are, sitting, waiting to hear from the doctor," he said, "when Jeff says he's not feeling too good and puts his head between his knees. Then he just keels over. Smacks his head right on the floor. Before I can go running off for help, Andrea kneels down and starts slapping him across the face, saying, 'Oh, come on, Jeff. Get up, will ya.' I guess it's happened before when he gets stressed out—he'll just pass out. I finally found a doctor and they put him on a gurney and took him to Emergency. He's got a nasty gash on his head but he's all right. Andrea took him home. I still can't believe it. Him lying there on the ground and her smacking him, saying, 'Get up, will ya.'"

"Oh my God," Elaine exclaimed, aghast at Dad's and my laughter. In our defense, Jeff would've only been offended if we *hadn't* found it funny. Out of all the family, his was the driest, most caustic sense of humor. It needed to be, for no way could anyone last the twenty-odd years he had been working at a funeral home by taking life too seriously.

We stopped briefly in the small third-floor waiting area to exchange hugs with the family. You'd never have guessed that's what we were to look at us, such a motley assortment did we present. Mom's barrel-chested brother Roger and elfin Aunt Alice, his wife. Mom's deceased sister Julia's four kids taking after their Italian father, all swarthy and burly. Claire so elegant and graceful, looking like a native Californian too, like Old Hollywood royalty, always dressed and groomed to perfection, never without pearls or a strand of her chestnut hair out of place. Dad with his glasses and stark-white beard and bald head covered in freckles, the only remaining evidence of the inferno-hued hair that had earned him the nickname "Red" growing up. Counting Melanie and Julia's kids' spouses, about a dozen people crowded the little room.

Dad then escorted me down the hall, around a couple corners, and through a set of automatic double doors. Just inside, as per the nurses' earlier instructions, he paused before a wall-mounted dispenser to sanitize his hands and insisted I do the same—as I would at least a thousand more times to come, before and after visiting her unit or room, always.

It took a moment or two for my eyes to adjust from the dim hallway to the incandescent unit. To the inside of the semicircular corridor were a nurses' station, storage closets, and an office or two; to the outside, half a dozen open-ended bays with retractable curtains at the mouths and a couple feet of maneuvering room to either side of the beds—even less in Mom's bay with the vent.

Despite Dad's forced insouciance, I'd steeled myself for a grisly scene, the kind I'd so often seen depicted in movies and on TV, especially what was lately Elaine's and Mom's favorite, *Grey's Anatomy*—Mom's face contorted in pain, sheets awry, gown besmirched by blood from the cath. What I found instead was the picture of serenity. Except for the breathing tube, the bed's thirty-degree incline, and the absence of a TV—which since the divorce she'd always kept on throughout the night—she might've been home asleep. She was a little pale, but her brow was unfurrowed, her jaw unclenched. A freshly laundered white blanket was pulled up to her shoulders and what little was visible of her gown was pristine. All this was even more unsettling than the gruesomeness I'd anticipated—Mom so innocent looking, so seemingly unaware of what had happened.

Later, after she was transferred to the Clinic, I'd get to be so hands-on the running joke was that I should be on salary. But right then I was so terrified of touching or bumping into anything that, as I leaned over the guardrail and kissed her forehead, I kept my hands shoved in my pockets.

"It's okay," I whispered. "I'm here. I'm right here. I'm not going anywhere. We're in this together. You and me. Same as it ever was. You keep fighting, okay? Keep fighting. Don't give up. I know you can hear me. I know you can. Keep it up. You're doing great. I'm right here. I'm not going anywhere. You're not alone. You hear me? *You are not alone.* I love you. I love you with all my heart and soul."

Out of the corner of my eye I saw Dad begin to sob, then leave the unit. I stayed a few minutes more. Before I left, her nurse handed me a plastic container—in it, Mom's watch, the wire-and-pink-gemstone necklace I'd given her a couple Christmases before, and Grandma's engagement ring, which after the divorce she'd had resized to replace her own.

IV.

I'm ashamed to admit that not only don't I remember the specifics about the heart attack—the percentage of blockage, if more than one stent was placed, her ejection fraction, what the hell ejection fraction even means—I never knew them all that well to begin with.

The lungs and digestive system I got good at, could explain, if rudimentarily, how the bronchioles give way to the alveoli, the duodenum to the jejunum to the ileum. And while the physics of radiation and chemotherapy were lost on me, I developed a decent handle on when one would be more applicable than the other. Drugs? Please. The way I came to be able to differentiate Ativan from Klonopin from Xanax from Compazine from Phenergan from Versed from Percocet from morphine—so far as they affected Mom, anyway— you'd have thought my last name was Merck. But when it came to anything heart-related, I was pretty much clueless.

I don't know how come. The oblong shape and asymmetry maybe, so unlike the linearness of the digestive tract and uniformity of the lungs. Or maybe it's just that there are so many components: six arteries, four valves, two atriums, two venae cavae, two ventricles. And an aorta. And a bunch of ancillary veins. (And that's the simplest diagram I could find on Google.) Or perhaps it's that comprehending the organ even on the most elementary level would make me incontrovertibly aware I have one inside me, working right now, this very second, and that scares the absolute shit out of me.

I e-mailed Melanie asking her to fill in the blanks. Her reply: *My recollection is that she had blockage in the left coronary artery, two stents put in*. Claire's journal—which she started keeping the day after the heart attack, a habit she'd got into from all the times Uncle

Max had been hospitalized, to keep track of the doctors spoken with
and all the medications and so forth as well as to provide an account
of the experience Max (and now Mom) might look back over later
on—confirms it was the left but only mentions one stent. Also mentioned is a balloon, which, come to think of it, I do remember—
though what its purpose was, again, I haven't the foggiest.

I suppose I could reach out to Dr. Cooper, the cardiologist who
performed the cath and placed the stent(s), and ask him to clarify,
but I'm not sure he'd remember. I mean, you'd think he would. He
himself had put her chances of surviving that first weekend at 5 percent, and for her to not only do so but to stabilize enough to transfer
to the Clinic—I can't imagine that's something he encounters every
day. And even if so, he had to have been astounded by how rapidly
she'd rebounded once there in Cleveland, which I'm guessing he'd
heard about from Anne, the ex-wife of one of Dad's nephews who
was a clinical nurse specialist and served as some sort of supervising
coordinator for General's ICUs. I think I even mentioned her progress myself in the card to the cheese-and-fruit basket we sent him
shortly after the bypass. But then, we also sent baskets to a couple
doctors who'd overseen her when she first arrived at the Clinic. Not
only sent them baskets, but, unlike with Dr. Cooper—who ad-
dressed the family as a group once, that first night, but to whom I
never actually spoke one-on-one—I'd discussed her condition with
these men at great length, shaken hands. And yet *they* didn't seem to
remember, not judging by how, after she'd been relinquished from
their care, every now and then we'd pass in a hallway or ride together in an elevator—or, once I'd found and started taking them,
on the stairs—and they wouldn't ask how she was, wouldn't say
hello or nod, wouldn't appear to recognize me in the slightest.

At first I took it as more than forgetfulness, as an extension of what I felt was the Clinic's absurd celebritizing of its physicians: the white coats with their names stitched on the breast, which I'd heard were laundered and pressed every night; the corridors lined with their headshots; the magazine and newspaper clippings in which they'd been quoted or favorably mentioned, framed and hanging in the hallway to the cafeteria. That two-hundred-odd-seat cafeteria was epicurean, featuring a Starbucks; the Mexican franchise La Salsa; a self-service breakfast buffet offering every kind of fruit, yogurt, granola, and pastry imaginable that, come noon, morphed into one of the most bounteous soup-and-salad bars you'd ever lay eyes on; hot entrée stations serving made-to-order omelets in the A.M., paninis for lunch, and for dinner everything from freshly prepared Caesar salad to barbecued ribs to baked tilapia; a smoothie station; a Subway open 24-7; and, incongruously to say the least, given the Clinic's choke hold on the number-one heart-care-hospital ranking by *U.S. News & World Report* (twelve years running in 2007), a McDonald's. Yet the doctors had a separate commissary whose spread I'd been told was ten times more various and gourmet, whose utensils and dishware weren't disposable, whose decor the one time I'd been walking past and caught a glimpse over the starched shoulders of a group of the initiated on their way in reminded me of the baronial dining halls I encountered at Oxford while there studying abroad junior year of college. All this intimated that interacting with a doctor outside the boundaries of your loved one's room or floor or unit—especially when the doctor was no longer assigned to your loved one's care—was a breach of etiquette equivalent to accosting a movie star on some Manhattan street for a photo or autograph.

Of course, it wasn't like I was trying to talk to them. Though I knew it was wrong, that they'd done everything they could've and should've to help her, that they *had* helped her, that if not for them she'd have been long gone, I couldn't keep from bearing them some measure of resentment, from holding them at least partially accountable for our still being there. And after a while, I realized these guys who possessed at least a dozen years of higher education could probably figure that one out; it wasn't their first time experiencing such radiating hostility; they weren't snubbing me but simply giving me a wide berth. That or they didn't think it was me but rather someone who looked like me, for never would they have imagined we'd still be there three months, six months, nine months, a full year later.

Now I see it differently still. Now I just figure it for absentmindedness. They just hadn't seen me, is all, had more pressing concerns than who the hell they were in an elevator with. In line with that, even if Dr. Cooper was willing to search through his records to answer my questions, I wouldn't feel right occupying his time. After all, if at the end of tending to Mom all day he'd then had to return to his office and dig through a bunch of old files and return some call or e-mail from somebody whose loved one was going on two years dead, rather than heading straight home and putting his feet up and having a cold one and thus arriving at work the next morning less refreshed, you can bet I'd have hunted that son of a bitch down.

The only reason she even had a 5 percent chance was thanks to Dr. Cooper's intrepid decision to use a cooling blanket, gone unnoticed by me initially from that white blanket on top of her.

With so severe a heart attack, there's the risk of the brain, kidneys, and other vital organs failing from lack of oxygen, as well as the part of the heart that's still in good shape giving out from trying to compensate for the impaired portion. Cooling therapy—a practice dating back to the 1950s and employed with some frequency in Europe yet largely neglected in America until a 2003 endorsement by the American Heart Association, and since then, according to a 2008 *New York Times* report, used only sparingly—lowers the body's temperature to around 90 degrees Fahrenheit, effectively sending those organs into hibernation and giving the heart some time to recover. After twenty-four hours, the temperature is then raised to normal, gradually, over a twelve-hour period. However, even were she to last that long, there was the chance she'd never regain consciousness, and if she did, still the strong possibility of significant brain and/or other organ damage.

That picture of serenity was a forgery. To be sure, over the next few days things would get awfully gory. Though still unconscious, she'd grow increasingly fitful, thrashing around until restraints had to be placed on not only her wrists but also her ankles. From edema, her arms and hands would bloat to twice their normal size. She'd cough up at least one clot that I remember—the blood gushing from the corner of her mouth and pooling on her pillow. And in case I still somehow underestimated the direness of things, I caught EMTs zipping up a body bag in the bay next to hers.

The thing that disturbed me the most, though, took place outside the hospital.

The third-floor waiting area was locked overnight, and so, as would be the case all weekend, that first night we spent in the more commodious, rec-room-like main-floor waiting area—Dad, Claire, Roger and Alice, Melanie, and a couple of my cousins in recliners

and on couches; Elaine and me on the room's six ottomans we'd
shoved against a love seat to form a makeshift twin bed. Next morning, after only a few hours' intermittent sleep—the ottomans constantly shifting and both of us a few times nearly falling through the
gaps—Elaine and I picked up Mom's Corolla at the health department and headed to the house to shower and change. Since moving
to New York, I only made it home a few days around Thanksgiving
and Christmas. The house would be spotless and stocked with my
favorite foods. It never occurred to me that Mom might live differently the other 350-odd days of the year.

Except for a box of cereal, a jar of peanut butter, and some cans of
tuna and tomato soup, the kitchen cupboards were barren. The refrigerator was only slightly less so—a few cans of diet soda, a couple
bottles of light beer, a box of soy milk, and a door full of condiments,
though besides a package of chicken cutlets little in the way of actual
food to put them on. A pile of dirty dishes lay in the sink. Reams of
opened and unopened mail were strewn on the counters.

In the living room the blanket usually kept folded in the front-
door closet was balled up in her TV chair. Nearby lay her sneakers
and socks. In the bathroom, the toothpaste, floss, and mouthwash
were out instead of stowed in the cabinet. In my bedroom, the mattress and pillows were stripped. In hers, as many clothes were on the
floor as hanging in the closet: a basket full of dirty laundry, another
of clean clothes folded but not yet put away, shoes everywhere, on
the chair next to the bed a mound of shirts and pants she'd tried on
then decided against, and, what really got me, on the bed itself—
unmade—her pajamas lying all in a tangle.

It wasn't just the thought that when she'd woken up she had no
idea what was in store that day; eventually I'd come to think she

very well might've and perhaps had been expecting it for some time. It was the loneliness. It pervaded the entire house. Only then did I begin to comprehend what a solitary existence she'd led since I'd left home. And it was no doubt thanks to this newfound appreciation that I took what happened that night the way I did.

A little past midnight, after assembling the ottomans, I went up to Mom's bay to say good night. To my surprise, she wasn't alone. At the foot of the bed stood a cop—mid-forties, black, with a handsome, clean-shaven face, a short fade, and muscles so enormous his uniform looked ready to split down the back Incredible Hulk–style any second. Despite his bulk, though, there was a docile aura about him. When I stepped to the side of the bed, he didn't ask my relation, didn't acknowledge me whatsoever, just kept staring at her with these warm, benevolent eyes

At first I figured he was some beneficent evangelical who every night, while his partner was over at the Krispy Kreme on Maple Street, spent his break in the unit going from bay to bay saying prayers for each patient. But when after five minutes he didn't move on, distraught and exhausted as I was, I started to wonder if I was the only one seeing him, if maybe this wasn't her guardian angel— really, not so far-fetched when you consider that manifesting as a cop with twenty-inch biceps is a hell of a lot more reassuring than *It's a Wonderful Life*'s old man in a nightgown or Nic Cage in that creepy *City of Angels* Columbine getup.

Then I had another, even more implausible thought: What if this was her boyfriend?

In the thirteen years since the divorce, she hadn't gone on a single date, had claimed no desire to. But what if she'd been lying? To protect me, no doubt, worried I'd have a hard time seeing her with someone. Granted, before that morning I probably would've. After finding the house as it'd been, though, I was enchanted by the idea.

I imagined he'd somehow got word what had happened—probably Mom had confided in Melanie, and she'd notified him—but, not wanting to add to the drama, waited till this late hour to stop by. Now here the two of us were, him wrestling with whether or not to introduce himself. I didn't want him to feel he had to, nor intrude on his time with her, yet wished to say good night in private should it be the last time I ever got to.

"Could you step out for just a second?" I asked him.

Even then he said nothing, just gave me a deferential nod and left the unit. I said a couple prayers and told her I loved her and that we were all downstairs if she needed us. I walked out the double doors expecting to find him, but he was gone.

"*Totally* Susie would be dating some hot black cop," was Elaine's reaction. She was the only one I'd told, in the event I really had been hallucinating. But then the next afternoon, while we milled about the main-floor waiting area in advance of our meeting with Dad's nephew's ex-wife Anne, he showed up again—this time in no less painted-on street clothes and alongside a coworker of Mom's. So much for my future stepfather. He was merely the coworker's husband, who, closer to what I'd first assumed, had stopped on his way home from work. I told them what I'd thought and we had a good laugh. Still, I was disappointed.

The process of raising her temperature was now complete, and so far there'd been no blood in her urine to indicate kidney failure. The next step, then, was reducing the sedation in order to gauge her responsiveness and determine if any brain damage had occurred. On this, her day off, Anne had offered to come in and discuss potential outcomes and options.

What would we have done that week without Anne? Walked around twice as fucking bewildered as we already were, that's what, as would soon enough be the case at the Clinic without her there to serve as intermediary—conferring with the nurses (with most of whom she was on a first-name basis) and paging Dr. Cooper ad infinitum, then translating it all into a parlance we could understand . . . and, when we still didn't, trying again.

That afternoon her patience was especially tested. Whatever Mom's ejection fraction—"a measurement of the capacity at which your heart is pumping," as defined on mayoclinic.com, which out of the Internet's surfeit of medical clearinghouses I found the most penetrable and comprehensive, even ahead of the Clinic's own site, and would come to consult on an almost daily basis—it was bad enough that Anne thought, were Mom ever to have a chance at getting anywhere near back to normal, probably nothing short of a heart transplant would do. At fifty-eight, she was still young enough to qualify. However, of the four thousand or so people perpetually on the national waiting list, only half can be accommodated each year. In the meantime, she'd need an LVAD, or left ventricular assist device. (*Grey's Anatomy* fans will know this as the thing whose wires Izzie cut in order for Denny to get the heart—so Elaine would later tell me.) Ten solid minutes we must've peppered Anne with questions as we struggled to wrap our minds around the apparatus's logistics and implications.

"It's an extremely uncomfortable way to live," she finally said. "I think you'd have to consider whether or not Susie would want that."

It didn't register at first, what Anne was driving at—not until she added there was no copy of her living will on file and we should make sure to bring one in.

Actually, Mom had just changed it a few months before, dividing the medical power of attorney between Claire and me—one of the things that leave me wondering if she guessed what was ahead. Then again, since it was Dad who'd previously held medical power of attorney, maybe it was something else. Maybe she'd reached the point where she was ready to part with that last vestige of the marriage and, even if not with her coworker's husband, try again.

Whatever instigated the change, dividing the power of attorney, Claire assured me, wasn't due to a lack of trust in my judgment—though I'd certainly given her enough cause over the years; Mom just didn't want me, if it ever came to it, to carry the burden by myself. I was grateful, and in fact—though my feeling about this would reverse itself in the end—a large part of me wished she'd left it up to Claire entirely. I doubted I was up to carrying even half.

A little after dark Elaine and I took a walk outside—just a couple blocks and back. The weather that weekend had been as pleasant as in New York those last couple days, but there was added to it that wistful fall feeling you only get all too fleeting hints of in the city. The hum of generators drowned out all other sound. We didn't talk. We just walked and held hands.

I'd gotten comfortable enough to take my hands out of my pockets and stroke her forehead. While doing so, I'd also talk to her. I can't remember what I was saying up there in her bay after my walk with Elaine. Maybe it wasn't what was said but simply the sound of my voice. Whatever the case, suddenly her eyes fluttered open.

I didn't want to cry, didn't want to scare her. But I'd yet to develop the kind of constraint I'd show upon seeing the newly installed G-tube. The tears streamed down my face. I continued stroking her head with my left hand while with my right I grabbed hers and squeezed.

"Hey there," I blubbered. "Hi, Mom. I love you. I'm right here. You're doing just fine. Just keep hanging in there. Everything's okay. Everything's gonna be okay."

Her pupils were so dilated they all but blotted out the irises. I put my face right up to hers but it was as if she were looking straight through me. Blank, vacant—it was horrible. After about thirty seconds, she slipped back into unconsciousness.

V.

Melanie and Dad each brought a cake that Monday morning to the third-floor waiting area. It hadn't been prearranged but proved prophetic, for my turning twenty-seven wouldn't be the only cause for celebration that day. Encouraged by how stable—how *alive*—she was, and to his everlasting credit humbly acknowledging the Cleveland Clinic's superior resources and expertise in the repairs he anticipated she'd need done, Dr. Cooper found a cardiologist there willing to take on her case.

We were elated. I wasn't sure how many years the Clinic had held the top spot in *U.S. News*, but so rarely did northeastern Ohio rank first nationally in anything other than population decline, I was aware it'd been a few, anyway. Whatever the outcome, at least there was no place she'd be better off.

That was the good news—the transfer had been approved. The bad was that currently no bed was available. And there was no telling how long the wait might be. A day maybe. A week. Maybe longer. In the meantime, of course, there was the possibility her condition would worsen and the move be called off. That made the rest of that day and the next two more unbearable than the first seventy-two hours. There'd been little reason to hope. Now there was—at least, there would be once she got to the Clinic. She just had to get there. *She just had to.*

"I'm so glad I got to spend my birthday with you," I whispered to Mom that night before leaving. In our three nights in the main-floor waiting area, Elaine and I had each gotten about twelve hours of sleep total. We figured if and when she got to the Clinic we wouldn't be getting much more and so decided, in those intervening nights, to try to get some decent rest. I didn't feel comfortable in the house without Mom there and wanted to be close to Dad, so we stayed at his place.

He'd bought the cozy ranch house with the detached one-car garage located just a mile and a half from Mom two years before, even more on the cheap than they'd gotten our house, though in its state of disrepair not nearly such a bargain. There was dingy gray carpeting and a three-inch film of dust throughout. The furnace was busted, the refrigerator and dishwasher shot. The galley kitchen was separated from the bordello-red, crystal-chandeliered living area by a sarcophagus-sized cabinet unit unsecured to the floor and likely to topple over at any moment—or, given Dad's luck, just as he was reaching in or walking past. Though they'd somehow manage to elude detection until that first winter I was back, a family of raccoons had commandeered the attic. All the same, it was a step up from that Valley apartment across from the driving range he'd rented since the divorce.

Not like I was there enough to know. In the four years before I left for Tampa, I spent the night in that apartment maybe six times and probably only crossed its threshold a couple dozen. After I'd been away for a while and the distance had given me the perspective necessary to resolve my issues surrounding the divorce, I'd think about that and it'd make me sick. It still does—the thought of Dad shopping for a bed for me or how the times I *would* stay he'd get up early and go to McDonald's so that there'd be a couple Egg McMuffins waiting for me when I got up, knowing they were my favorite, wanting to do anything he could to make me feel more comfortable. Only child or no, how could I have been so selfish, so insensitive? How did it never dawn on me that maybe he didn't like being there any more than I did, and that the only thing that gave him any solace was having me around? Could I seriously not give him just one lousy night a month? Every two months? Hell, every six?

No. I couldn't. I was thirteen. I hated it. Hated that he didn't have cable. Hated that to change the channel with his remote you couldn't just punch in the numbers but had to then hit *enter*. Hated how poofy his couch's throw pillows were. Actually, it *was* pretty cool the times he'd forget his keys and would boost me up so I could scale the wrought-iron second-floor balcony and go through the sliding door he always kept unlocked for that very purpose. But that was only a few times. Otherwise we'd use the front door, and I *really* hated that—the possibility of running into one of his neighbors and the embarrassment I'd feel over hearing them say how much he bragged about me. Thirteen.

Again, time and distance would help me get over that bullshit—just as being back home for as long as I was, along with my long hair and love for basketball, would to some degree resurrect it—but I continued to despise that apartment.

For one thing, living in New York made me realize for the first time just what it meant to live in an apartment—waiting days for the super to get around to fixing your plumbing, neighbors asking you to turn down your music, you having to ask the same of them, hearing their footfalls, their fighting and fucking. In your early twenties was one thing, but I hated the thought of my fifty-something father having to put up with that crap.

That and the absence of a lawn. As much as he loved basketball and golf, by far his favorite pastime was yard work. Perhaps the reason I took so much pleasure in looking at Mr. Angeletti's garden is that it reminded me of Dad's mowing, edging, watering, weeding, raking, aerating, fertilizing, and twig collecting. The only grass at the apartment complex, meanwhile, were the small patches along the front walkway maintained by the management company.

That was what sold him on the ranch house—if the inside was a dump, it was likely because the previous owners had sunk all their time and money into the backyard: tulips, azaleas, roses, daffodils, elephant grass. Best of all, it being a corner lot, he had twice the front yard of his neighbors.

By the time of Mom's heart attack, he'd gotten the place looking as good inside as out. He'd had the carpeting ripped up and amber hardwood laid, the walls painted cream, the furnace and appliances replaced, that cabinet monstrosity taken out so that the living area and kitchen were transformed into a lodgelike great room. And he bought all brand-new furniture: a large mahogany dining table; two armchairs; the couch he'd picked up with Mom; various side tables, lamps, and rugs; a desk and bookcase for the office room. The only thing he didn't bother getting was a bed for me. Instead, in the second bedroom he placed a futon. After three nights on those ottomans it was the most comfortable bed both Elaine and I had ever slept on.

My memory of the rest of her time at General is poor.

There was the coughed-up clot and the thrashing and the rest.

There was the security guard. Since Friday—and who knows how long before—there'd been a bundle of dirty linens in the corner of the third-floor waiting area. By Monday it had started getting rank. There were no windows in the room, so to air it out we propped open the door with a chair. An elderly security guard with a huge gut came by and said we couldn't block the hall like that. It was a fire hazard.

We gave our reason and asked if he could then get housekeeping to come clean up the linens.

"That's not my job," he said, and pushed the chair back into the room.

"We're just going to put it back when you leave," I said.

He glared at me. I glared back. He left. I put the chair back. We never saw him again. No one ever came to pick up the linens.

There was the night walking through the lobby that I ran into a girl I'd been friends with at Litchfield Middle School. It had been almost ten years since I'd seen her. She was pregnant and there with her mom for a birthing class.

There was the night Elaine, Sully, and I finally had enough of brought-in pizza and decided to treat ourselves to a good dinner. It was almost ten and all that was open was the Summit Mall Ruby Tuesday's. We were the only people there. I got a steak. Elaine got the salad bar. Sully got the sliders. How can I remember that but not how many stents?

One afternoon in the hallway outside the third-floor waiting area I hugged Melanie as she wept.

"It's all my fault," she said.

"It is not," I said.

"Yes it is," she said. "I knew she'd been having trouble with her asthma lately. I kept telling her to go to the hospital but you know your mom. It seemed to clear up but then last week started up again. I should've taken her to Emergency. I should've strapped her ass in the car and taken her to Emergency."

"Like you could've," I said. "You said it yourself. You know how stubborn she is. And you know she'd be fucking pissed if she knew you were blaming yourself."

Melanie laughed.

"Yeah," she said, and sniffled and wiped her eyes.

"So don't," I said.

One afternoon a priest from St. V stopped by at Claire's request. I can't remember if he'd come to perform the Anointing of the Sick as he later would at hospice or to simply pray over her.

She opened her eyes for Uncle Roger once. I can't remember if she opened them for anyone else. She didn't for me again.

*　*　*

Wednesday morning the call came. The plan was to transport her to the Clinic around seven that evening by helicopter. I'd be allowed to ride along. I'm embarrassed to admit it, but I was excited. I'd never ridden in a helicopter before.

It was sunny and clear all day. I hadn't seen the forecast, but nobody said anything about a storm. Then around five it began turning overcast. By six the sky was completely gray and it was starting to get gusty. By seven, though it had yet to rain, the winds were gale force and it was so black you couldn't see but for the occasional flash of lightning.

The helicopter was coming from some other hospital. There was a half hour of phone calls back and forth about whether or not they'd be able to fly in such conditions. Finally it was decided to take her by ambulance instead. To organize this was a process. By eight o'clock, Melanie couldn't stand waiting any longer and set out. Dad, Claire, Roger, and Alice left about fifteen minutes later.

There wasn't enough room for me to ride in the ambulance. Since Sully was more familiar with Cleveland, he offered to drive Elaine and me up in Mom's car and have his mom pick him up. It made me sick to leave Mom at General alone, but I wanted to be sure I was at the Clinic when she got there. A little after nine, then, after I'd kissed her and told her I loved her about a dozen times, we left.

It still hadn't started to rain by the time we reached 77. Then halfway to Cleveland the sky all at once opened up. I'd never seen rain like it, even my freshman year of college when Tampa got pummeled by El Niño. Car after car was pulled off the road with their hazard lights on. The Corolla's wipers were on the highest setting but might as well have been off for all the good they did. Sully was unfazed. I don't know if it was his police training or what, but he kept it steady at the speed limit and didn't hesitate to pass more cautious drivers.

She's supposed to die, I remember thinking from the backseat. She's supposed to but she won't and God's going to make that ambulance crash if that's what it takes.

CHAPTER THREE

I.

While I now consider it a dank cubbyhole, St. V's gym, my CYO team's home floor—with its dot-matrix scoreboards, pull-out wooden bleachers, and glass backboards that retracted from the ceiling—was to my ten-year-old self nothing short of palatial, especially next to the grade school's across Market where we practiced. That court's dimensions were three-fourths regulation, its backboards wooden, no more than a foot between the baselines and brick walls. The sideline out-of-bounds wasn't much wider, plus it had the added danger of the stainless-steel cafeteria counter because the gym doubled as lunchroom during school hours; bruised shoulders were as common as rolled ankles. There was no place to sit except a small staircase leading to an equipment closet, and during scrimmages score was kept with flip-over numbers. Yet inconceivably, before the current gym was built in the fifties—with money raised from candy bars sold by my parents and uncles and aunts and the rest of the then grade and high school students—it was here that the high school played its games. And in that era, there was no St. V player—no player citywide, as family lore has it—more dominant or heralded than my grandfather, Mom's dad, Arthur Hesidence, class of '28.

I never got to meet him. He died of a heart attack at sixty-four, six months after he and Grandma moved to Fort Lauderdale and six years before I was born. Still, he was always more familiar to me than Dad's dad, whom I also never met. This was due to Grandpa Hesidence's being said to have been a dead ringer for Bing Crosby, and so every Christmas when *Holiday Inn* and *The Bells of St. Mary's* would come on I'd imagine him crooning "White Christmas" or rescuing the school from insolvency. Also, Mom and Dad simply spoke more of him than of Grandpa Manning: how he could fall asleep anytime, anywhere; how he always wore a tie, even around the house; how when not napping he'd cloister himself in the basement of that drafty, falling-down Crosby Street four-bedroom/one-bath just a few blocks west of the church slaving away on his inventions; how his talent on-court had made him as much the toast of the town as LeBron would one day be.

Neither Claire nor Roger remembers his position. Lithe and average in height as he appears in photos, I'd peg him for off-guard, small forward maybe. He earned a scholarship to play at Wittenberg University, a tiny Lutheran college in the southwestern part of the state, but only lasted one year. Then the Depression struck and—this remains unclear—either the scholarship was rescinded or he was summoned home to help support his siblings and widowed mother.

The Depression hit Akron particularly hard. As related in the definitive 1999 history *Wheels of Fortune: The Story of Rubber in Akron,* by 1932 the city's industrial unemployment rate reached 60 percent, or almost three times the already staggering national level. Grandpa, however, was awash with job offers—the rubber companies and other area corporations hot to add such a ringer to the starting fives of their competing employee teams.

Grandpa went to work for Goodrich. He'd stay there for more than a decade, first in purchasing, then sales. This was a rarity—going straight to a cushy desk job without serving time in the factory. But then the bosses would be reluctant to see their prized recruit's fingers chopped off in a splitter—which often happened, according to Dad, who'd worked the tire-treading machine when he started out.

"Other men who had the talent took Samuel's tricks and sold them and grew rich, but Samuel barely made wages all his life," John Steinbeck writes of the Hamilton family patriarch in *East of Eden*. He could just as well have been describing Grandpa Hesidence. He was always coming up with product ideas, most notably a garden hose punctured with tiny holes to serve as a whole-lawn sprinkler. It was a huge moneymaker but patented in the name of the company, and Grandpa received only a dollar for his part. After other such slights, he left Goodrich for a stint at General Tire and then, upon finding himself just as ill-used, another at Marathon Oil before finally, in his mid-forties and with Mom just a few years old, going into business for himself.

Like his son-in-law, Grandpa was even more accomplished at golf than at basketball—having led St. V's linksters to the 1927 state title, the school's first in any sport. (This only made my hacking more vexing.) He created a swing-training device as well as an early version of the indoor putting mat. Only for these two have I been able to track down patents, but Mom claimed he also came up with the clip-on bag towel.

Thanks to his reputation, he was able to place the items with local retailers. They sold moderately well, and employee wages weren't a concern thanks to the kids and whatever family and friends made the mistake of arriving early for Sunday-night penny-ante poker. Even so, with the material costs, patent fees, and everyday household expenses mounting, Grandma had little choice but to go to work, in the credit department at Polsky's.

World War II rejuvenated the American rubber business, and the baby boomers' subsequent fixation with the open road, abetted by 1956's Interstate Highway Act, kept it thriving—until the early seventies, when surging oil prices, massive inflation, endless disputes between the equally culpable heads of labor and management, and Detroit's shift from bias-plies to radials felled the industry. Then came the Japanese takeovers of the eighties. Then the widespread layoffs of the nineties, which would claim Dad, after thirty-four years with Goodyear and one shy of his full pension. From six-figure ad exec to minimum-wage courier for the county school system— and thankful, nearing sixty in northeastern Ohio's tanking economy, to find any work at all.

By the time I was a kid, it was hard to believe my parents' assertions that downtown Akron had once been as bustling as the opening scene of *A Christmas Story;* that every December growing up they and their friends stood with their noses pressed against the lavishly decorated display windows of Polsky's and O'Neil's; that those two department stores had been engaged in a rivalry as fierce as that between Macy's and Gimbel's in yet another of our holiday film favorites, *Miracle on 34th Street.* For that glass that had then showcased BB guns and toy trains was long pasted over with for-lease signs, the same as in nearly every other South Main Street storefront. By the time I was a kid, folks did their shopping in the neighboring city of Fairlawn, at Summit Mall—or their loitering, as in the case of my friends and myself, who in middle school would spend entire Saturdays doing loop after loop without entering a single store.

Sometimes driving to and from church or basketball practice, Mom would take Crosby instead of Market, and it'd be just as tough to envision a time when there weren't ratty couches on porches and boarded-up doors stamped PROJECT HAPPEN to signify a raided drug house—a time when, by how she described it, doors were gratuitous, so commonly were they left open to facilitate the constant comings and goings of the many neighborhood kids, their sounds of play filling the air as densely as the smell from the factories.

Much of that clamor owed itself to her. Though she always ascribed her tomboyishness to being closer in age to Roger (two years) than Julia and Claire (nine and eleven years older, respectively) as well as a dearth of neighborhood girls, surely that reversal of roles—Grandpa at home all day, Grandma out being breadwinner—had something to do with it. There's a black-and-white photo dated '52 of her in the backyard posing before a pup tent with Roger and a neighbor boy, all three shirtless in dungarees and homemade headdresses, bows and quivers of arrows slung over their shoulders. She loved playing jacks; when I was six or seven, she taught me on the kitchen's linoleum floor and could still pick up tensies with ease. At the calling hours, a man from the old neighborhood quipped to Dad she'd been by far the fastest of all the kids. Dad got the biggest kick out of that. Weeks later he'd still keep bringing it up.

If the whole *Miracle on 34th Street* contention was hard to swallow, there was no disputing her uncanny likeness to the film's star, little Natalie Wood. In her late teens and early twenties she began to even more eerily resemble Ali MacGraw. The Hesidence girls were all stunners. Claire, a former majorette, did some modeling that landed her a few local TV appearances. For a time Julia was a stewardess with TWA. Mom, with her raven-black hair and aquamarine eyes and figure fit from all those footraces, was thought by many to be the prettiest of all.

It was around then, while she was in high school, that Claire and Julia began having kids, and Mom always made herself available to babysit. But that was the limit to her responsibility: Though she looked like a silver-screen ingenue, her behavior was closer to Janis, Mick, Sly, and the other rock stars whose albums were among her most prized possessions. She ditched class, smoked, dated like crazy—especially after Roger shipped for Vietnam and all his buddies who'd for years been pretending not to notice her swooped in. Everyone but Dad, who between college, work, and taking care of Grandpa—the reason he was spared combat duty—was genuinely unaware of her existence.

II.

Mom never protested my affinity for hip-hop. Granted, she wouldn't let me buy albums with parental-advisory stickers till high school, but that was of no concern. Gangsta rap had yet to monopolize the genre and there were still plenty of high-minded emcees who escaped Tipper Gore's wrath. Too many. No way could my ten-dollar-a-week allowance—a fortune, really, considering all I did for it was take out the trash, the only chore Dad ever left me to do—cover the gargantuan shopping list I compiled every Saturday morning during

BET's *Rap City* countdown. In eighth grade, then, I took the caddy test at Portage, one of the nation's oldest country clubs, founded in 1896 by the first Goodrich executives and to this day, more than a century later, the epicenter of Akron's elite.

By the time I found my way into catering, I'd worked enough shit jobs to appreciate one whose sole duty was to walk around handing stuff to rich people who acted as if you didn't exist. At twelve, though, with no professional experience, I thought that sort of thing beneath me. I showed up to the caddy yard every morning for a week and caught a loop or two, then stopped going. I had that luxury, unlike Dad.

Lured by the obscene glut of jobs the advent of the automobile had bestowed on Akron, aspiring laborers and their families from points all about the globe grew the city's population from just north of seventy thousand in 1910 to two-hundred-thousand-plus a decade later. One of these was a teenager from Cadiz, Ohio, named Clark Gable. Another, a teen from Clarksburg, West Virginia, named Catherine Yost. Truthfully, Dad's not sure when exactly Grandma arrived with her seven siblings and newly widowed mother, nor how long it was before Grandpa, then just her sweetheart, followed. My guess is not until the Depression. It would explain Grandpa going to work for a dry cleaner rather than in one of the factories.

The cleaners provided the setting for some of Dad's earliest memories. It was located behind St. V's modern-day gym, on Green Street next to the football field. Back then there was no locker room for the visitors. So they spent halftime in the shop. Grandpa was in charge of supervising and often brought Dad along. Dad loved the sight of the players in their uniforms and dreamt of the day he'd wear one.

It was a dream never to be realized. He stopped growing even before I would and was thought too scrawny by St. V's coaches. Since he'd been the star quarterback on all his grade school teams, this was a massive disappointment. (Having still not fully gotten over it by his freshman year at U of A, he decided to walk on. It took about forty-five minutes for the equipment manager to locate a pair of pants small enough, and just one more for Dad to observe the ferocity of a tackle drill and promptly hand them back in.)

It was on those grade school teams that he became friends with Roger, who was two classes behind. While by his own admission failing to inherit Grandpa Hesidence's athletic prowess, Roger did acquire his father's work ethic and entrepreneurial spirit, and at just eight years old began making the three-mile round-trip trek between Crosby and the Portage caddy yard.

Dad had a paper route and so wouldn't join him there until high school, when Grandpa's declining health and work hours demanded greater supplementary income. It was uncertain what ailed him— CT and PET scans were still years off—until late in Dad's freshman year at U of A, when throat cancer was discovered. (Smoking was judged the cause, but Dad maintains all those dry-cleaning chemicals contributed.) His larynx removed, bereft of speech and saddled with a trach—Dad's acclimation to the sight of which would allow him to take Mom's much more in stride than I would— Grandpa was unable to work at all.

Dad was even more of a latecomer than Mom. Fourteen years separated him from his eldest brother, who after a time in the navy settled in California and had a family of his own. Another brother, ten years older, lived in Akron, but he too had kids and was struggling enough to provide for them. And Grandma had to stay home caring for Grandpa.

Caddying those last three years had helped ease the financial burden, but no way would it be enough in itself to sustain the three of them, especially not with tuition and medical expenses. That's when Dad sent the letter to Vic Holt.

Holt was what might've become of Grandpa Hesidence had he been willing to play ball figuratively as well as literally. According to his 1988 *New York Times* obituary, in 1923, as a six-foot-seven senior, he led the University of Oklahoma basketball team to an undefeated season and was honored as that year's most outstanding collegiate player. After helping one of the Sooner State's AAU teams to two national titles, he was brought to Goodyear to shore up the employee team frontcourt, then climbed the company ladder until eventually becoming president in 1964.

He was still just a vice president when one afternoon a couple years earlier he'd teed it up at Portage and drawn Dad as his caddy. What a surreal sight that must've been—Dad's flaming coif flopping and the bag of irons jangling as he rushed to keep up with the towering executive's immense stride. Holt shot his lifetime low that round and requested Dad on the bag for the remainder of the summer. By its end, he was asking after Dad's career plans and offering a leg up.

When Dad sent the letter inquiring if the offer still stood, he doubted Holt would remember him. Two weeks later he was working the eleven-to-seven graveyard shift in Plant 2 as member of the B squad, filling in for whatever A squad regulars called off, a different assignment each night—though always smearing his face in petroleum jelly beforehand so the lamp black would be easier to get off.

That was 1965. Dad was twenty-one. He wouldn't be elevated out of the factory until 1969. By then he'd lost his father, graduated college, and been dating Mom two years.

III.

Despite palling around with her brother, their concurrent hitches in grade school and high school as well as the countless Sundays and days of obligation the two of them spent beneath that same ceiling inscribed with the cardinal virtues, and never living farther than seven blocks apart, Dad claims the first time he laid eyes on Mom was his senior year at U of A, when she was a freshman. Though I can't say for sure, I imagine she noticed him before. With his features, he was hard to miss.

Mom and Grandpa Hesidence aren't the family's only cinematic doppelgangers. In his indistinguishableness from Woody Allen—the slight build, glasses, by his late twenties dulled-to-auburn and rapidly thinning hair—Dad exacted the most double takes. Sure, nowadays there are few less flattering comparisons to make of someone. But back in the sixties and seventies, when Allen (himself called Red as a boy) was a bona fide sex symbol, gracing magazine covers from *Time* to *Esquire* and bedding Diane Keaton, the parallel was leveled as a compliment. "Your dad always looked great in a suit," I remember Mom saying, and what she loved most about his job—ahead of the robust salary and his trips to Paris, Japan, and other far-flung destinations that brought her all sorts of keepsakes—was that it mandated he wear one every day.

True, they were complete opposites. He loved music, too, but Sinatra, Paul Anka, Andy Williams—unlistenable dreck to her. About the only artist they agreed on was Cat Stevens, whose recording of "Morning Has Broken" inspired them to use the song for their wedding processional. He'd never been tempted to smoke, and naturally was even more averse after Grandpa's throat cancer. She would quit during pregnancy, but by then was up to two packs a day. She found it much easier to give up school, leaving after just the one year at U of A and taking a job Grandma had gotten her at Polsky's. Again, even while at Goodyear, Dad had followed through on his degree.

But then, as antithetical as disparity is to friendship—what made Sully's and mine so remarkable—it's precisely what fires romance. She saw in him the discipline and responsibility she then lacked; he saw in her the rebellion and impetuousness absent from his own life. I totally get that. What I don't, what I never have, is how in the world she agreed to a second date after what happened on the first.

"It could've been worse," she'd always say when I was little and had suffered some embarrassment that'd gotten me crying. "Like your father on our first date. Sitting there at that nice restaurant eating dinner. He takes a bite of food and I say something that gets him laughing and all of a sudden a pea shoots out of his nose! A little green pea—right back onto the plate!"

That's my dad: Not only did he once look like Woody Allen, he also shares the comedian's propensity for pratfalls.

In a single weekend ski trip to Pennsylvania when I was nine, his poles flew off the roof while on the highway; when he went to hand the turnpike ticket to the tollbooth attendant the wind swept it out of his hand and he had to pay the maximum amount; and on our very last run, as he paused midway down the hill to adjust his goggles, he was upended by a kamikaze ninety-year-old man who was on skis for the first time ever and didn't know how to stop.

Even the bleeding ulcer he suffered around that same time wasn't without a measure of hilarity. While out at lunch with a friend, he suddenly passed out. Rather than falling off to one side or toppling backward in his chair, he keeled face-first into his bowl of soup. And if a little dignity couldn't be permitted him for one of the gravest events of his life, you know for one of the happiest it *definitely* wasn't.

Playing in a pickup game a couple days before the wedding, he caught an elbow to the face that left him with a nasty black eye. For the ceremony he wore more foundation than Mom. If only that'd been the worst thing to mar the occasion. Dad had been adamant about using a priest he was friendly with from U of A. St. V, though, wouldn't allow outside clergy. So instead of being married where they'd both been baptized, received first communion, and were confirmed, they were left to use St. Peter's across town.

That wasn't all. The reason Grandma and Grandpa moved to Fort Lauderdale was to keep their sister-in-law company after Grandpa's brother unexpectedly passed—word of which came *an hour* before Grandpa was to walk Mom down the aisle. He still did, but left immediately after for the airport. Whenever Mom would tell the story, even twenty, thirty years later, she couldn't keep the dolefulness out of her voice. I believe before her inability to have more children or even the divorce, that was her life's single greatest disappointment: not getting to dance with her father at the reception, especially since he himself would pass within the year.

Well, at least she had the honeymoon to look forward to. Where would it be? The Caribbean? Hawaii? Mexico? Somewhere warm, certainly, it being the middle of November.

Try Colonial Williamsburg.

As a kid, of course, I thought that had to be the coolest honeymoon ever—buggy rides, glass blowing, everyone in costume. At what age exactly I came to realize tavern ale by candlelight wasn't as amorous as poolside daiquiris by moonglow, I can't remember. But whenever it was, I asked Mom what gave.

"Your father liked history," she said. He'd majored in education and would've gone on to teach high school had he not been granted refuge from the factory shortly following graduation.

"You mean it wasn't a money thing?" I asked. By that fall of 1972, after rotating a month or so at a time through Goodyear's various divisions—a practice meant to help young employees find the field best suiting them, since, unlike today, there was every expectation they'd remain there until retirement—he'd found his niche in advertising and was serving as a senior copywriter. She was still at Polsky's—three years yet from her job in the claims department at Social Security. Their incomes combined, they were by no means doing badly—just not well enough, I'd figured, to afford a more opulent excursion.

"Nope," she said, "that's just something he'd always wanted to do."

IV.

The less-than-storybook beginning wouldn't be spelled by their first apartment. That Fourth of July, the man who occupied the bottom floor of the northside duplex stood in the street firing a shotgun into the air in celebration. "It was a couple days after that your mom started looking for a new place," Dad says. In the deal she found on the house, her luck finally changed.

Because of its precipitous terrain—the city is the seat of Summit County, called so in recognition of the highest point on the old canal, while its own name derives from *akros,* Greek for "high"— Akron is full of treacherous streets. There's Sand Run Parkway, which, traversing an outlying portion of the Valley's federally protected area, fords a stream and in heavy rain is closed to traffic; vertiginous South Bates Street, more commonly known as Cadillac Hill, that area boys sled down in winter; Tallmadge Parkway, in the sixties renamed Memorial Parkway after a fierce rainstorm collapsed the sewer beneath, opened up a giant crater in the road, and swallowed a car whole, resulting in the death of a ten-year-old female passenger and two men who tried to rescue her. On Portage Trail, I once watched a passing car hit a patch of black ice and veer into an oncoming vehicle, killing the driver. My friend Paige was killed upon losing control of her car on a twisting, humpbacked stretch of Merriman Road and striking a tree. And less than half a mile south of there is Lafayette Drive.

Although not quite as steep as Cadillac Hill, banking sharply before the crest, Lafayette and its slippery red brick was far more perilous, especially in the snow. At the crest itself was a tiny concrete bridge beneath which ran the old Akron, Canton & Youngstown railroad. At least once each winter a car crossed the bridge, failed to make the turn, and ended up in the front yard of the topmost house. Ascending the hill was even more problematic: 677 Lafayette was halfway up, right about the spot where, momentum flagging, cars would start to struggle, tires to spin and smoke. On snow days or

Christmas vacations, I'd spend hours from my perch on the back of the couch beneath the living-room picture window cheering the tenacity of some drivers and booing those others who too quickly let themselves roll back down to try again.

That you took your life in your hands most every time you came or went from our house was in part why Mom and Dad were able to snatch it for a song. Primarily, though, it was the awkward size: The fifteen-hundred-square-foot, two-bedroom, two-and-a-half-bath split-level with partial basement was too much house for a single person and—though the location was ideal, just a few blocks from King Elementary, arguably the best grade school in the district—not nearly enough for a young couple bent on having kids.

Which Dad, in light of his upbringing, was not.

King, for a bit of trivia, was the site of the first Alcoholics Anonymous meetings. And while on the subject of intemperance, I've agonized whether or not to mention Grandpa Manning's. I'm not concerned about opening old wounds—though that certainly would've been the case were this a few years ago, before Dad started going to Al-Anon and opening them himself. I simply don't want Dad to think that's the first or only thing I think of when it comes to Grandpa. In fact, it's the last. I think of what a talented drummer he was, how he'd earn extra money sitting in with swing combos at area dances. How he loved to fish, and how when Dad was still in the house he'd kept Grandpa's old wooden pole mounted in the rec room.

When finally I came clean about my apprehension, Dad insisted I do mention it.

"That disease was part of who he was," he said. "There's nothing shameful in it. To leave it out wouldn't be paying him appropriate tribute."

One of those halftimes in the dry cleaners would stand out most of all. Unhappy with his players' performance, the visiting coach was really laying into them, sparing no obscenity. Dad was stunned—not because he'd never heard such language but because it was the first time he'd ever heard it coming from anyone other than his father.

That opening scene in *A Christmas Story* wasn't the only one famil-iar to Dad. Grandpa was acid-tongued in his inebriety—a virtual Rembrandt, following Ralphie's description of his own father's having "worked in profanity the way other artists might work in oils or clay." Ironically, the larynectomy would reduce him to exactly that—using ink and paper to dispense his vitriol.

"Your father was worried because of the environment he grew up in he wouldn't be any good with kids," Mom once confided to me. "But I knew he'd be wonderful."

She'd told him as much herself, but to no avail, so that, still child-less six years into marriage, she was finally compelled to employ a more artful strategy. There to greet Dad one evening upon his re-turn home from work was a sad-eyed, long-eared, black-and-white-mottled springer spaniel puppy. Designed to conjure his nurturing instincts, the plan almost worked a little *too* well—soon Dad was showering more affection on Patches than on Mom herself. He'd be the one to bathe the dog in the utility-room sink, lie flat on his belly trying to coax her out from under the bed where she'd scurry in fright during thunderstorms. Our first home movies—shot on Super 8 and, when I was little, screened in the living room using a projector and pull-down screen—are of Patchie bounding through the snow. Dad even had the three of them sit for one of those classic Olan Mills nature-backdrop portrait photos.

Nonetheless, the plan worked. Mom was pregnant within the year. Just to be sure there was no further confusion of priorities, she placed my crib in the exact spot in the living room where the dog normally slept.

CHAPTER FOUR

I.

So as to distinguish it from its satellite locations and specialization offshoots in Toronto, South Florida, Las Vegas, and—coming in 2012—Abu Dhabi, as well as Fairview and several other area affiliate hospitals, the Clinic's flagship—forty or so buildings spread over 140 acres just east of downtown Cleveland—is called the Main Campus. Intentional or no, it's particularly apt for a teaching hospital with both an on-site university—the Lerner College of Medicine—and a research division employing more than twelve hundred scientists and adjutants. And there were other ways still the place felt at times closer to a college than a hospital.

At the cafeteria, staff paid by swiping their ID cards rather than using cash. The private police force had its own uniforms and cars. Shuttle buses ran between the various buildings and parking garages. Smoking was prohibited anywhere on the grounds, but the ban was dodged by patients (under the cover of the city bus shelter just outside the main entrance) and employees (in their cars) alike. With its name plastered on the southwest corner gate of Cleveland Browns Stadium and the left-field wall of the Indians' Jacobs

Field—excuse me, now *Progressive* Field, the auto and home insurance company having paid $57.6 million in 2008 to have its name
slapped on the side of the ballpark for the next sixteen years, the exact
same amount it would have cost to treat Mom plus twenty-three
others in her identical condition—and the Cavs' practice facility, the
Clinic even gave the impression of having its own athletic teams.

Then there was the main entrance.

For the same reason the starting point on prospective student and
parent college tours is always the campus's most hallowed building—
be it U of A's pediment-happy Buchtel Hall or the University of
Tampa's minaret-topped Plant Hall—the Clinic's main entrance
was intended to engender trust, allay fear, promote tranquility, emit
refinement, and, above all, conceal the chaos and profaneness truer
to its character.

The ruse began before you even reached the entrance. The pas-
sageway running beneath Euclid Avenue and linking to P1, the
Ninety-third Street parking garage, was lined with this strange
plastic that looked pink from a distance but as you went changed all
different colors, a kind of chromotherapy meant to calm you, lessen
your dread. From there you traveled up an escalator and into the
entrance's grand foyer, its ceiling some thirty feet high, its walls for
much of the way all windows. From the daylight reflecting off the
marble floor (waxed and buffed nightly), it managed to be brighter
inside than out. Beyond the windows to one side lay, in warm months,
a bed of red tulips and a man-made brook that, through a pane in-
laid in the floor, could be seen coursing underfoot as you passed into
the hospital proper. To the other side, through a set of automatic

sliding doors, was a circular drive into which, further propagating the air of civility, black-tied attendants valeted from P1 those vehicles belonging to families of newly discharged and still wheelchair-bound patients. These patients were themselves chauffeured into the lobby by a transport-team member, identifiable by their light green polo shirts. Even more conspicuously garbed in red sport coats were the greeters, whose job it was to provide directions, bid you good morning and afternoon, generally act perky, and otherwise combat your trepidation.

After threading this gauntlet of courteousness and passing into the hospital, you came up against a half dozen or so large oil paintings of past presidents, all looking long on sagacity, sitting in their book-lined offices, legs crossed with massive tomes resting in their laps. And should this corridor, complete with dim lighting and dark wood paneling, prove *too* staid, it was immediately followed by another functioning as art gallery: four or five large abstract paintings, rotating every couple of months, with the artist's name, a short biography, and a brief statement of intent stenciled on the bright white walls.

Only then, after a couple quick turns, did you arrive at the H Building. This a good ten minutes after leaving your car. If they couldn't rid your worry by dissembling, they'd exhaust it out of you.

Our being there as long as we were, it was only a matter of time before I realized all this was indeed a ruse. It was inevitable that the curtain be pulled back. I just wish it hadn't had to happen on first setting foot in the place. It would've been nice to be oblivious for a little while anyway.

*   *   *

Dad was just getting out of his car as we pulled into the garage. We were both able to get a spot on the ground level. The tollbooth was unstaffed. There was no one to tell us where to go. The rain came down now harder than ever.

"It's gotta be those glass doors down at the end of the block," Sully said from where we stood just inside the garage's entrance.

"That'd be my guess," Dad said.

"Could it be that door with the little staircase?" Elaine said.

"I'm saying the glass ones," Sully said.

"You'd think it being the Cleveland Clinic and all they'd make the entrance a little more fucking obvious," I said.

But that's not what we were looking at. Just as Dad had, we'd made the mistake of coming in on Carnegie rather than Euclid, followed the signs for parking, and picked the first garage we'd come across, P3, on Ninetieth Street.

We decided on the glass doors—what was a back entrance to the radiology and oncology offices, a destination we'd eventually come to know all too well—and made a run for it. With the wind, the rain fell almost horizontally, pelting us in our faces. Finding the doors locked, we ran to the door with the staircase, but that wouldn't open without an ID swipe. Drenched, we ran back to the garage to phone Claire or Melanie. Just coming out as we got there was a young girl with an umbrella, her unzipped jacket revealing a maroon smock the same color as her pants.

This was yet another way the Clinic advanced the illusion of order: Every job had a color-coded uniform. Red sport coats for the greeters. Light-green polo shirts for lift team as well as transport. White polo shirts for food services. White scrubs for nurses, kelly green for aides, royal blue for respiratory therapists, red for phlebotomists, black for physical therapists, and gray for X-ray and other machine techs. Even the stitching on the doctors' coats was a signifier: Attending physicians' names were black and in cursive, those in training—from residents to fellows—blue and in print. Maroon was for housekeeping. We told the girl we were trying to get to the H Building. Rather than point out our blunder and the way to P1, she offered to escort us.

Going in through the employee entrance, chilled and wet, navigating a seemingly endless maze of narrow back hallways crudely lit and cluttered—at times to near impassibility—with broken beds and other in-need-of-repair equipment as well as carts overflowing with both clean and dirty linens, peeling paint, exposed and clanging pipes, the sound of a radio, the trading of good-natured epithets, laughter, and then just like that through a door and into the spaciousness and decorum and hushed calm of the H Building: This was *my* first impression of the Cleveland Clinic's Main Campus. And while it did, regrettably, lay bare the place's dualism its dichotomy of authenticity and artifice, it also revealed its capacity for kindness. The girl from housekeeping's graciousness would be as much a harbinger of our time there as would the irregularity of our entrance.

II.

In most every way H-22 was twice that of General's third-floor ICU. The bays were twice as large and enclosed by glass instead of curtains to offer twice the privacy. In Mom's bay at General, there'd been one small window offering a less than spectacular view of a pebbled roof and exhaust vents. In her H-22 bay, one whole wall was a picture window that looked onto Carnegie. There wasn't any more equipment—unless you counted the TV suspended from the ceiling at the foot of her bed (which I most certainly did, knowing again how much comfort she always took in having it on at home)—but it looked doubly sophisticated. And whereas the majority of the nurses in the General ICU were fairly young, on average in their late thirties, most in H-22 were nearer to Mom's age.

Of course, that was no guarantee they were twice as seasoned—like her, they could've come to nursing late—and, in fact, I can't say as I ever learned any of their names let alone how long they'd been on the job; our time in the unit was too short—too *smooth*—to cultivate the sort of rapprochement I'd later have with the G-53 and reSCU staffs. But such abundance of experience was certainly the sense I got, and right from my very first trip into the unit. The deftness with which the pair of nurses worked as they finished getting her situated, the way they handed instruments and supplies and charts to one another unprompted, their movements so instinctual and harmonious: It was balletic.

Light on their feet as the nurses were, there was still plenty of noise and bustle. Yet the only acknowledgment from Mom was the gelatinous wobble to her skin whenever somebody brushed against the bed. Two visitors were allowed at a time. By the time we'd all had a chance to see her and ask the nurses our fill of questions, it was well past three. Elaine and I had arranged to stay with my friend Ben, he of the Cavs-game ticket mix-up, who lived in one of the old machining factories converted into trendy lofts a few blocks from Browns Stadium. The rest of the group had booked a room at the InterContinental Suites.

* * *

There were three hotels on the Main Campus. The smallest—the seventy-four-room Guest House—was operated by the Clinic. The two others—the seven-floor, 144-room InterContinental Suites and the nine-floor, 299-room InterContinental—were run by the eponymous chain. The largest was arguably the most exclusive hotel in the city. One of the reasons was its restaurant, Table 45, which would open that spring of 2007 and be named one of *Esquire*'s top twenty new restaurants for the year. Nothing can convey what a paradoxical, ass-backward town Cleveland is better than that, not even the over-polluted Cuyahoga River catching fire in the late sixties: For a delicious meal and fun night out, you go to the hospital.

When we arrived, the Guest House was closed for remodeling. As an alternative, set up catty-corner from the main entrance on Euclid and Ninety-third were a half dozen FEMA-style trailers, available for about a hundred dollars a night. In one of these was a lady from Buffalo.

She was around Claire's age, small and thickset, with glasses and short, blond hair. Her husband had had a heart attack similar in severity to Mom's and was flown in from a hospital in Buffalo six weeks earlier. According to her, he was no better off than he'd been there, and by the end of our time in the unit she'd begun demanding the doctors transfer him back. She didn't care what it meant for his chances.

"Six weeks!" we all kept saying. "Can you imagine being in the hospital *six straight weeks*?"

We being not just our group but the other families we became friendly with in the H-22 waiting area. (Ten by ten and with no reading material except for a couple decade-old *National Geographic*s and a hardback copy of Tina Turner's autobiography, the space didn't leave us much of a choice.) There was a local woman, in her early sixties, whose husband was in. Always with her was their thirty-something daughter and her year-old baby girl who never stopped smiling. And a woman in her early forties who was also a native but now lived in San Francisco. It was her mother. After a few days, her husband and twin teenage boys flew in. I can't recall what was wrong with her mom, but she expected it to be the last time the boys saw her.

It's these people I remember more from those first days than what was going on with Mom. That's because not much was. In Claire's journal, all that's mentioned from Thursday till Monday is that her doctor had something come up that required him to transfer her to the care of another, she'd begun to open her eyes a little more and seemed more responsive to our voices, and the thrashing continued: She was so strong she broke one pair of wrist restraints. For Friday, Claire didn't even bother making an entry.

No, that first weekend at the Clinic it wasn't Mom I had to worry about. After that first night at Ben's, Elaine and I spent the next couple back at Dad's. Sunday she was flying back to New York. Since the flight wasn't till late afternoon, Dad went up at the start of visiting hours and let us sleep in. After seeing Elaine off I'd come and relieve him. That was the plan, anyway.

When Dad got to the hospital he started feeling light-headed and noticed some pain in his left arm. He told one of the H-22 nurses, who advised him not to take any chances and go to Emergency. He was heading there when he called me. Have I mentioned my father's like Woody Allen?

I can joke about it now, but at the time I was plenty scared. After all, it wasn't as if there was some cosmic dispensation that, because of Mom being how she was, meant the rest of us were exempted from illness or disaster. (At least I didn't think so at the time.)

Elaine and I found him a couple hours later tucked into a tiny, curtained-off corner of the ER, shoes off, sitting up in bed eating chocolate pudding and watching golf on a little swivel TV. An EKG had been normal, but just to be safe they wanted to keep him overnight and do a stress test (which he'd pass) in the morning.

I hated to see Elaine go. Having my girl there had indeed made me less prone to lose it, but not in the way I'd expected—compelling me to play the part, act tough. Rather, Elaine gave me whatever strength I had. Her back rubs and back scratches, the famous hand massages that Mom herself would in time so savor. Just the way she'd look at me—her seeing me as so capable of handling it all made me believe maybe I was. Plus, with that one-of-a-kind Dominican-Comanche complexion and shampoo-commercial hair and those big brown eyes, she was something exquisite to gaze upon amid all the infirmity, the sight of so many illness-ravaged bodies and grief-deformed faces. Hated to see her go. Hated the prospect of staying by myself that night with both Mom and Dad in the hospital.

We cut it too close for me to park and walk her into the airport, so I had to just drop her off outside. We kissed and hugged, and she promised to come visit in a couple weeks. She would—and every two or three weeks after that for the next fourteen months.

Monday it looked as if Elaine might have to turn around and come right back for the funeral. Another catheterization had been scheduled for early Monday afternoon. The hope was to remove some blockage and possibly replace the stent(s) or add more. A few patients needing caths even more urgently kept pushing Mom's back. A little before five, one of the unit's fellows called us from the waiting area into a small office. (Actually, it wasn't till a couple days later that I realized he was a fellow. Though younger than both her first and present doctors, he was so no-bullshit and take-charge that I automatically judged him for an attending. I'd yet to learn about the jacket stitching.) Dr. Leonard was his name—mid-thirties, blond buzz cut, thin. I'd continue seeing him around the hospital in the months that followed, but whenever I did I would always duck behind the nearest corner. I suspected from how he'd treated us that unlike those other doctors he *would* recognize me and say something and perhaps, just perhaps, blame himself for our still being there, for how dire things had turned out. Preferring to let him imagine everything had worked out fine, I hid.

There in that little office, all of us sitting around a conference table, Dr. Leonard explained that over the last hour Mom's blood pressure had out of nowhere bottomed out and that they were about to rush her into the cath lab.

"The odds she'll survive are fifty-fifty," he said. "There isn't much time for questions. I just wanted you to know so that if there's anything you want to say to her—"

Before he'd even finished I was through the office door and into her bay and at the side of the bed leaning down over her, kissing her, telling her I loved her and not to be scared while nurses scrambled all about me, moving equipment out of the way to make it easier to wheel the bed out.

She was in the cath lab for over an hour. Dr. Leonard sat with us for a half hour more explaining the outcome and answering our questions. They hadn't been able to remove any blockage and could now say with certainty the stenting wasn't going to do the job long-term. They had also discovered some internal bleeding from the original cath site inside one of her thighs. That's why her blood pressure had plummeted. They were going to start giving her blood to see if that made any difference.

It didn't take long to find out. Tuesday she was more responsive than ever, gave Claire a wink. By Wednesday night she was alert enough to watch TV and even try to communicate. I couldn't tell what. She was still intubated and restrained even though the thrashing had finally subsided. (At its worst, Dad and I had stood to either side of the bed holding her hands so that when her arms flailed, her wrists wouldn't get any more lacerated.) She pointed at something in front of her. I went to the wall and pointed to the clock.

"The time?" I asked.

She shook her head and kept pointing. I pointed to the assignment board.

"Your nurse?" I asked. "You want your nurse?"

She shook her head, pointing furiously now, eyes bulging.

"The date?" I asked.

Her hand fell to the bed. She closed her eyes and shook her head. I went back over and started stroking her forehead.

"I'm sorry," I said. "Let's keep trying. I'll get it I will."

She shook her head and went back to watching the TV. I wanted to cry. I felt so useless.

When I came into the bay the next morning the bed was at a 90-degree angle and the restraints were gone and instead of being intubated she wore a breathing mask over her nose and mouth. Does it seem sudden, the way I just dropped that on you without prefacing it with something like, "Then Thursday, walking into the bay I got the biggest surprise of my life," or "Thursday, walking into the bay was the happiest moment of my life"? Multiply that by a thousand and you'd just begin to get a sense of my shock. When she saw me, she waved. Just like that. Waved. Like it was no big deal.

To her it wasn't.

Claire had gotten there before me. She'd brought a pen and a spiral notebook to see if maybe Mom could write.

She tried a couple of times then printed SEAN! What a moment!! She also wrote WHAT HAPPENED . . . I told her she had a heart attack, possibly from Hodgkin's chemo. She printed WOW. She printed NOT ASTHMA . . .

"Asthma?" I asked when, done smothering her with kisses, I saw what she'd written. "What, you thought you had an asthma attack?"

She nodded. The oxygen hissed loudly as it traveled from the wall through the thin plastic tubing attached to the mask. The mask was clouded by vapor from the breathing treatment she was receiving. Some escaped and billowed around her head.

"Did you know you were in the Cleveland Clinic?" I asked.

She shook her head, rolled her eyes, and threw up a hand in disbelief at her ignorance. She didn't remember a thing—not opening her eyes that Sunday night in General, not me telling her not to be scared before the recent cath.

"What about last night?" I asked her once the mask was off. "You remember what you were trying to tell me?"

She said something but her voice was less than a whisper. I put my ear right up to her mouth and she tried again.

"Beer?" I asked. I looked at the wall. It still took me a second. "Oh, there was a beer commercial on TV!"

Again she rolled her eyes and threw up her hand.

III.

About the chemotherapy, Claire was mistaken—radiation instead had been used to treat Mom's Hodgkin's lymphoma. Nowadays doctors typically treat the disease using chemo and/or radiation shot with pinpoint accuracy at the cancerous area—the type she'd receive for her lung. Back when she was diagnosed in the early eighties, protocol had been radiation alone, on large swaths of the body. Along with the risk of birth defects in future offspring, another side effect was asthma. So she was told. What doctors weren't aware of at the time—and what's only started coming to light in the last few years—is the damage such imprecise radiation can do to the heart. Her trouble breathing, it seems, wasn't from asthma so much as congestive heart failure. In fact, the Clinic doctors speculated she never even had asthma.

I could never remember how old I'd been when she was diagnosed. I'd thought one, maybe two. But then cleaning out her bedroom closet, I found a bunch of old paperwork from Social Security, including a year-end performance review that listed her four-month sick leave as beginning in November 1983, just after I'd turned four. "You are an inspiration to many, including myself," the reviewer wrote.

Her wig was wavier than her real hair, not as dark and shorter than ear-length, as she'd by then taken to wearing it. She kept it on a Styrofoam head on a shelf in her bedroom closet. Grandma Hesidence spent a lot of time at the house helping out with me; conveniently, she'd moved back from Fort Lauderdale just months earlier. Since Dad had to work, Julia drove Mom to and from radiation. She'd always bring garbage bags, and Mom would throw up the whole ride home.

I asked her about it once, one of those Thanksgivings or Christmases home from New York. I was sitting at the kitchen table finishing the beer I'd had with dinner while she rinsed the dishes and loaded them into the washer. I forget what we were talking about that led me to ask and what she said in reply. It wasn't much—"It was really rough," or something like that—so I dropped it.

She wasn't any more forthcoming about *why* she wasn't more forthcoming, but I gather it was a combination of reasons. It just wasn't her to dwell. Unlike Dad, who's an analyzer, an *agonizer*—his collection of self-help books as vast as his array of lob wedges and lawn equipment—Mom just accepted things and moved on. Not to say she didn't sorrow. One time in seventh grade I barged into her bedroom to find her sitting on the edge of the bed sobbing. When I asked what was wrong she said she was just thinking about Grandma. This was a couple of years after she'd passed. Until then, even at the funeral, I hadn't seen her shed a tear. She sorrowed, all right, but never wanted to burden anyone else with it.

Especially not me. I imagine that was her foremost incentive for downplaying the Hodgkin's—wanting to protect me, shield me from life's brutality and unfairness and pain. Also, I firmly believe, she never wanted being a cancer survivor to be her identity the way it is for a lot of people. The last few years she'd participated in the American Cancer Society's twenty-four-hour Relay for Life fundraiser walk at an area high school, but she didn't go for wristbands or ribbons or bumper stickers. She'd much rather be thought of as a good mother, a good sister, aunt, friend, and colleague. A good nurse.

*   *   *

She'd been at Social Security a little over eight years—"Development Clerk" is the job description on her review, "Claims Clerk (Typing)" on her official resignation form, also among those papers in her closet. There are a couple photos of her at her desk, which looks identical to the twenty or so others in the unpartitioned office: two-slot mail sorter, a dozen file folders standing upright in a wire organizer, totally eighties punch-button phone, nameplate, baby-grand-sized typewriter to her left so that she had to turn her chair to use it.

It was a good enough job. Located in the federal building down on the corner of Market and Main, it was a five-minute commute. Since it was civil service, the benefits and security were excellent. And she made a lot of close friends; after she left, she'd still go to dinner with a group of them once a year. But it didn't have her jumping out of bed in the morning; in fact, in another performance review predating her illness, she was chided for being late seven times in a single month.

Getting sick not only made her realize the importance of doing something she really loved, it also showed her what that something was: nursing. I can't say for sure what specifically brought about the epiphany, if it was one particular nurse she had during the radiation who inspired her or the lot of them. Hell, knowing her, they could've all sucked and that could've been what did it.

Dad offered to pay the cost of school—by then he'd risen to advertising manager of Goodyear's aerospace division—but she refused, had to do it for and by herself. It was another four years at Social Security before she'd finally amassed enough in retirement savings. Then she quit and cashed that in and in the fall of 1988, at forty years old, more than twenty years after dropping out, went back to U of A full-time.

I went with her to the old Gardner Student Center to buy her books for that first semester; she got so annoyed at how few used versions were in stock. In the rec room was an old desk that had once belonged to Grandpa Hesidence, but she preferred studying on the bed; I can still see her cross-legged and hunched over, reading with her different colored highlighters laid out next to her, can still see the drawing of Zeus on the cover of her Cliff Notes for mythology. We took turns running flash cards for each other, and most days she packed herself the same lunch as me. At commencement, while waiting for the ceremony to start, she blew up a surgical glove into a balloon and batted it around with her classmates like a beach ball.

That was December 1992. A member of three honor societies, she didn't have to send out many résumés. By the following April she was working for the health department, one of ten or so nurses, Melanie among them, assigned to home visits.

She spent each day, usually by herself, driving a city-owned car around the more destitute sections of town—including the Crosby Street area—following up on little kids suffering from lead poisoning or congenital defects, taking their vitals and drawing blood, making sure they were keeping up with their medications, and offering referrals. The average was six visits a day, but one day, with the help of another nurse with whom she'd been paired, Mom set the record: twenty-five. ("We were all so pissed," Melanie says.)

It was an emotionally trying job, seeing nothing but hard-luck families all day long. On top of it she had to come home to me grousing about leftovers for dinner or her refusal to buy me an additional pair of batting gloves for baserunning only. One day she'd finally had enough and took me with her.

We made about eight visits. The last was some east-side public-housing complex. There were four or five brick units, three floors apiece with doors opening directly to the outside. She was checking on an elderly shut-in. I forget what was wrong with the woman, but she had an oxygen tank of the same sort I'd hook Mom up to in reSCU when taking her outside in the wheelchair. The whole apartment couldn't have been bigger than our living room.

I got the message. But what I really took away from that day, more than a grasp of others' travails and our comparative good fortune, was what a terrific nurse she was. It wasn't just the command she showed when discussing drugs and dosages or her adeptness with a needle, but the way her patients all brightened upon seeing her—upon seeing me, too, for they'd all heard so much about me. Of course, this embarrassed me no less than running into Dad's apartment neighbors. However, I realized that such sharing of herself wasn't just motherly pride, that it was as integral to her work—to doing it *well*—as anything found in her over-the-shoulder supply bag. She knew it wasn't an easy thing, these people opening their homes to a total stranger, letting her minister to them or their loved ones. Having been poor and sick herself, she was sensitive to how hard, how humiliating that might be. So in return she let them into her life—just as the best of the Clinic staff would let me into theirs.

CHAPTER FIVE

I.

They kept her in H-22 till Tuesday, October 10. An ultrasound had found a clot in one of her legs. To prevent it from traveling to her heart or lungs, a tiny filter was inserted into one of the venae cavae to catch it if it broke free. Also, it was determined there was more leakage in one of her valves than originally thought. So while she qualified for transfer to a step-down floor, as long as her bay wasn't needed for a more critical patient, the doctors preferred to keep her in the unit where everything could be more closely monitored.

It was hard to believe watching her improvement in those intervening days that things had ever been so bleak. She began to eat. (. . . *mashed potatoes, fish, spinach, rolls. She devoured— except for the spinach.*) Though still gravelly, her voice was coming back. Her urine foley and fecal tube were removed and, with help from the nurse or myself, she was getting out of bed to use the portable toilet.

She wasn't as pleased by this as the rest of us. Because her heart was so weak, it had trouble processing all the fluids she was being given—the antibiotics and other IV medications as well as all the Diet Sierra Mist she was sucking down. This was what caused edema, and the fluid building up in the pleural space—the cavity between the lungs and the thorax—made it difficult to breathe. To help take it off, she was being given Lasix, a diuretic, and had to get up and go at least once every hour. Even the annoyed faces she'd make about it, though, were a good sign, meant she was getting back to her old self.

Things continued to improve once in that private, ninth-floor step-down room where we'd watch the Cory Lidle crash coverage—so much so that I finally felt comfortable staying at the house by myself. She was out of bed and sitting in a chair for an hour or so at a time. She'd even begun to walk. I'd stand to one side of her, Uncle Roger or a nurse to the other, and, holding onto our arms, she'd go a little farther each day—first to the door and back, then halfway to the nurses' station, then all the way.

Again, as Dr. Leonard had made clear to us, the stenting wasn't a long-term solution, and so it wasn't a question of if she'd need bypass surgery but when. The step-down doctors advised she go home, spend some time getting stronger, and come back—they were projecting she could be discharged as early as that weekend. We found that preposterous. She still needed to be helped out of bed, wasn't fast enough to make it to the bathroom, still used a portable toilet. She lacked the strength and balance to take a shower. Forget stairs. And what if she had another heart attack? She was already in the hospital—why not just go ahead and do the bypass?

It was then that we remembered Aunt Julia's niece by marriage who, up until a few months before, when she and her family relocated to Columbus, had worked as a nurse for one of the Clinic's top cardiovascular surgeons. We called her to see if she might ask him to consult, and a couple hours later Dr. Martin showed up in Mom's room.

His staff page on the Clinic site was novella length—teeming with fellowships, directorships, principalships, adviserships, professorships. He specialized in dozens of diseases and conditions and more than fifty services. He'd helped develop the first FDA-approved artificial heart and performed its very first implantation. A Google search showed him having coauthored publications with Dr. Mehmet Oz of *Oprah* fame. Much later, Melanie would send me an article she happened across in a national woman's magazine in which he was credited with performing a valve replacement that brought to an end a woman's nearly two-year struggle to resolve her chronic fatigue and shortness of breath. His is the one framed headshot I specifically remember seeing in the halls—thick, slightly mussed black hair a bit graying on the sides and a wry half smile, as if incredulous he's being asked to pose for a photo amid all his other demands. And if all that weren't impressive enough, he couldn't have been fifty.

While Dr. Martin conceded it'd be unwise to send Mom home, time wasn't so of the essence that the proposed valve repair and double bypass—using a mammary artery and one from her leg—couldn't be put off a week for her elevated white-blood-cell count to come down and her blood pressure, low as of late, to go up. Because of an opening in his schedule, it wound up taking place a couple days earlier than that, on Tuesday, October 17. He predicted she'd be home by Sunday—officially one month since the heart attack.

II.

Still another way the Clinic felt like college was the class loved ones were required to attend during the surgery. It was held in a tiny windowless room on the upper level of the P Building's colossal surgery-center waiting area. There was a chalkboard, a couple dozen small writing desks, even a text—a three-ring binder two inches thick with bullet-point handouts on what to expect as well as worksheets and checklists all separated by tabs into sections labeled "Before Surgery," "During Your Hospital Stay," "Hospital Recovery," and "Recovery at Home" and offering such pearls of wisdom as

> *If you have a hearing aid, please wear it the day of surgery so you can hear and understand everything we need to communicate with you.*

> *Don't hesitate to inform the health care professional if you think he or she has confused you with another person.*

> *Eating good foods is an important part of healing.*

and my favorite

> *It may take time to return to an active sex life—create realistic performance expectations . . . . [and for] the first six to eight weeks, use positions which limit pressure or weight on the breastbone or tension on the arms and chest.*

A DVD was included as well—though whether or not it offers a demonstration of those positions, I can't say. It was in with the notebook, get-well and sympathy cards, Dr. Graham's business cards, little notes from Elaine I'd find in the car or house after dropping her at the airport, and the rest of the detritus I can't bring myself to throw out—still sheathed in cellophane as when it was passed to me that day in the class. Rather than page through it and furiously scribble down the instructor's drivel along with everyone else crowding the room, I sat there with my arms crossed, sulking. The whole thing smacked of a teammate mentioning to his pitcher he had a no-hitter going, and though I doubted the gods who adjudicated baseball also held jurisdiction over medical matters, I figured it best not to participate and make an obvious display of my abstention just in case.

Fortunately, the class only lasted a half hour. The rest of the day we spent with our nails dug into the arms of our lower-level waiting-area chairs—out of nervousness but also necessity, for if we hadn't clung to them so, there was a good chance they might've been swiped out from under us. I didn't notice a single seat empty or at least not vigilantly guarded. I couldn't find the statistics for 2006, but in 2007 the Clinic performed 3,438 open-heart surgeries, or roughly ten a day. That Tuesday I'd guess there were no fewer than fifteen families waiting.

What a well-oiled machine it was. On one of the upper-level walls were departure-and-arrival-style monitors listing every patient and their status—whether still being prepped, on the heart-and-lung machine, or out of surgery and headed to one of the five cardio-thoracic ICUs. Those same buzzers you get while waiting for a table at Ruby Tuesday's or Applebee's were used to notify the family when the doctor called the reception desk to inform the designated spokes-person—in our case, myself—of the outcome.

Mom had gone into the operating room a little before noon. She was placed on the heart-and-lung machine a few minutes past three.

Dr. Martin's call came just after six. There had been no problems. I wasn't on the line with him but fifteen seconds yet managed to get off a half dozen thank-yous.

We weren't allowed to see her in the G-53 ICU for a couple hours yet. In the meantime, Roger treated everyone to dinner at the Inter-Continental's antiquated, white-gloved-waiter dining room that would be shuttered within weeks to make way for Table 45. Instead, I grabbed something in the cafeteria. Though the final out had been recorded, it still felt premature to celebrate.

G-53's half dozen or so beds were an arm's length apart, separated by curtains. There was no room for even a folding chair. There was no need for one. Visiting hours were ten to eleven thirty, four to six, and eight to nine, and you could only stay for durations of fifteen minutes. Tiny TVs attached to the ceiling by swiveling metal arms kept patients company the rest of the time. Standard following surgery was one night. Mom's blood pressure was running low, so she was kept two.

Early Thursday afternoon, just ahead of when she was scheduled for transfer, her bed was moved into the center of the unit so the bay could be given to a patient fresh out of surgery. Because of some ad-ministrative snafu, it was another five hours before the patient whose place Mom was supposed to take in the tenth-floor step-down unit—her fourth unit in three weeks—was finally discharged. Five hours with no curtains, in plain view of other patients' visitors, no TV, no call button. Her voice still faint and unable to be heard over the alarming of vents and infusion pumps and the rest of the unit's tumult, she had to raise her hand to get the attention of a nurse or aide. By the time I arrived, she'd grown so frustrated that she'd started crying. I spent the next five minutes lambasting the unit co-ordinator. Five minutes after that transport arrived in their light green polo shirts.

Aside from that, though, things went smoothly for a week and a half following the bypass. (And even that incident turned out fortu-itous, as I harangued the ombudsman into giving her a private room in recompense.) Her appetite was good, she was walking with as-sistance again, she was doing strength-improving exercises with a physical therapist, and, most momentously, with the help of a student nurse she took her first shower since the heart attack, one day shy of five weeks. After an ultrasound showed no signs of clots, the filter was removed.

The only thing keeping her in the hospital was her blood pres-sure, which continued to run low and prevented her from receiving the standard post-op heart meds whose effects needed to be moni-tored prior to discharge. By Wednesday, October 25, her pressure had stabilized enough to begin the Captopril and Coreg, and the consensus was she'd be home no later than Monday, just a week be-hind schedule.

III.

At five thirty that Sunday morning, Mom called Claire complaining she'd been up all night nauseated and vomiting and asking her to come up. (She didn't call me because Elaine was in and she didn't want to infringe on our time together.)

Got there about 7:30. Sat with her, laid in bed with her. She fell asleep for a few hours. Still was not right. I asked to page Dr. Martin's service . . . two of his residents came down. Her stomach was very distended. Wanted to put tube down her stomach and take her back to ICU on the fifth floor . . .

I remember Claire calling to let me know Mom was returning to G-53, but draw a blank on how the rest of that day went. Same for the seven days that followed—other than the one night she was boiling with fever, writhing and moaning, and every couple minutes I'd refresh the cold washcloth on her forehead by dunking it into a plastic measuring cylinder full of ice water. Which, I suppose, says just how much fucking agony she must've been in, especially given all the other ghastliness I remember too well: that coughed-up clot in General; the scare a couple weeks after she moved back to G-53; the time not long after that when the doctors were struggling to put in a new central line (a sturdier, more permanent IV with multiple ports) and I came back into the unit expecting them to have already finished and saw the sheets covered in blood and the gaping hole in the inside of her thigh; the time in reSCU I did the same thing, walked back into her room before they'd finished replacing a central line, to find Kevin the RT on one side of the bed helping keep her turned and the doctor on the other boring away at her neck.

She just never had any luck with central lines. They'd always get infected—this was how her veins got so shot, requiring her to instead rely on peripheral IVs. According to the journal, it was in that week that her very first central line was placed, just below the right collarbone, so that she might receive TPN, or total parenteral nutrition, a type of intravenous tube feed. It'd been three or four days since she'd eaten. Or gotten out of bed. Too weak but also hampered by a urinary-tract infection—one of at least a dozen she'd contract, the stinging and spasming during urination excruciating, causing her to grit her teeth and cry and squeeze my hand with all her strength. The staff doctor wanted to remove the foley until the UTI cleared up but Mom insisted it simply be replaced with a clean one; Lasix had been started again and she didn't want to bother with a bedpan every ten minutes. Lasix was increased to twice a day, then three times. Still she struggled to breathe, was for a day or two placed on the breathing mask as well as subjected to multiple pleural taps. In this procedure, performed at the bedside, a needle is inserted into the back, between the ribs, and any fluid is extracted. One tap removed an entire liter.

Then, a week after being readmitted to G-53, she began to complain of abdominal pain. Though a CT scan would later prove negative, a problem with her appendix was feared, and in the event surgery was necessary she was intubated and moved to one of the two adjacent, glassed-in rooms at the rear of the unit—what the nurses called the X-Box, since those assigned to each were also responsible for the bay diagonally across.

Roomy and enclosed, a regular-sized TV suspended from the ceiling, and a picture window with a view of Carnegie: Her X-Box room was a mirror image of her H-22 bay. And yet the two couldn't have felt more different. Her H-22 bay seemed airy. The X-Box was stuffy and dismal. No doubt this had much to do with the X-Box's remoteness within the unit after her having been in the center of H-22, directly across from the nurses' station. And then there were the circumstances. H-22 we'd always associate with things getting better; G-53 with their going to shit.

But to what I'd most attribute the two rooms' contrasting dispositions is the time that had elapsed. In northeastern Ohio, there's no greater change in the weather and concomitantly the mood than between early October and early November. The leaves that had then been so resplendent, the vibrant reds and oranges and yellows, were now fallen, withered, brown. No longer was there the chance for the odd 60-degree day; the cold had set in for good. That wistfulness I'd felt out walking with Elaine the one night at General was replaced by gloom. More than the leaves or temperature, though, it was daylight savings that did it, that cast this pall. It began getting darker and darker earlier and earlier—what good is a picture window when it's overcast all day and pitch-black by five? In yet another of those uncanny confluences, the day the clocks were turned back— Sunday, November 5—was the very same she moved to the X-Box.

Thanks to Mom's *New Yorker* gift subscriptions, I was familiar with Dr. Atul Gawande's writing on physicians' fallibility, how they're no less error prone than the rest of us. And that merely confirmed what I already ascertained from her own stories about work, such as one of the nurses accidentally sticking herself with a needle used for an HIV test. No, if anybody knew better than to think medical professionals irreproachable, omnipotent, anything more than human, it was me. But appreciating this in the abstract is one thing; being confronted with the reality of it quite another.

Take my attitude toward Dr. Martin. Again, the timing made it impossible not to correlate the nausea and vomiting with the bypass. However, fluid drained from around her heart by chest tubes gave no indication of heart failure, nor did repeated echocardiograms. While still very weak, her heart clearly wasn't the culprit. The surgery had been an unequivocal success. Dr. Martin had done his job.

It would've, then, been within his rights to leave her in the hands of the G-53 doctors. Yet until she transferred to reSCU, and even for the first couple weeks after that, he continued to check on her three or four times a week, often showing up well into the evening, just out of surgery, still in his white cap and utility pants and short-sleeved button-down. In addition, he had personally called on some of the Clinic's finest specialists to consult. They were all just as stymied as him, granted—it wasn't till a couple months after being in reSCU that we'd hear the term *gastroparesis* and the intubating/extubating posit, nor till then that the gastric emptying test would be conducted—but even that was to his credit: how he didn't try to conceal his bafflement. Unlike one G-53 pulmonologist who'd claim with near certainty it had somehow to do with the Hodgkin's, that Mom's body was just taking longer to recover from the shock of the surgery and that it was only a matter of time before it righted itself and the nausea and vomiting stopped. Dr. Martin had more respect for us than to offer such empty reassurances, was never anything but on the level, even more the man than his staff page on the Clinic Web site had made him out to be. And *still* I grew embittered with him. *M— stops by,* I wrote in Claire's journal on Monday, November 6. *Doesn't have many answers. What's new?*

That night Melanie came up after work with an absentee ballot for the midterm election. Hardly necessary given Mom's card-carrying liberalism, Melanie still read off each of the candidates' names. Mom gave a thumbs-up to the ones she wanted. Dad helped steady her hand as she signed.

Tuesday she rebounded a bit and was able to be extubated. It wasn't twenty-four hours before she was once more struggling to breathe and intubated. Wednesday, a CT scan of her chest suggested pneumonia, perhaps from aspirating vomit or not being out of bed in so long or both. Later that same day, to get a better look, a bronchoscopy (or "bronch") was performed—almost identical to the pre-incision portion of the G-and-J-tube procedure, only using a slightly different scope and passing it through the trachea on into the lungs rather than through the esophagus to the stomach. The bronch showed a large mucus plug definitively indicating pneumonia. It also showed, as noted by Claire, *an old clot or something*. Whoever performed the procedure had been without the necessary scope attachments to remove the plug and biopsy the something, so another bronch was done Thursday.

I didn't concern myself much with the biopsy. The results weren't expected back till the following week. Who knew if she'd still be alive? Despite the removal of the mucus plug and a barrage of antibiotics, the pneumonia remained unabated, her system further compromised by an infection in her central line. Her blood pressure dropped and soon she was back to that comatose thrashing; this time the restraints included padded mittens. Then there was the drama of Monday, November 13. More than at any other time so far, more than during the H-22 cath even, I thought for sure we'd lose her then.

As far as I could tell, she was in no better shape than she'd been in the last few days, had shown no sign she was ready to breathe on her own, but whoever was the G-53 staff doctor—they rotated every week or two, as would be the case in reSCU—thought differently. I left to go to the waiting area while the extubation was taking place but didn't get ten feet before an alarm started going off in the room. Her nurse rushed past me. I hurried back in. The tube was still in but Mom's eyes were now wide open, staring up at the ceiling. Her chest was heaving. The monitor above her head clocked her heart rate at 140 and climbing. Her nurse returned with another nurse. The first was carrying what looked like a couple large adhesive bandages. The second nurse helped roll Mom toward the door. The first peeled off the backing on one of the bandages and stuck it between Mom's left shoulder blade and spine. The two of them rolled Mom onto her back and the first nurse tugged down the front of Mom's gown and stuck the other bandage over her heart. I had just noticed the bandage had a couple small leads when another nurse came in and beckoned me out of the room. I stayed put.

"What's happening?" I asked.

"Everything's okay," she said. "Just go on back to the waiting area."

"No," I said. "If she's going to die I want to be here with her."

"You're in the way here," the third nurse said. "Come with me."

She led me through a door along the rear wall of the unit, into a small hallway where supplies were kept. She promised that if it looked like Mom wasn't going to make it she'd get me. For fifteen minutes I tried to pray but couldn't concentrate. How would it work? What would they do with her after? How would we get her back to Akron and Jeff's funeral home?

Finally, the nurse returned.

"She's okay," she said. "She just got scared when they went to take out her breathing tube and her heart went out of rhythm but they got it back. Trust me, it looked a lot worse than it really was."

The bandages had been defibrillator pads. They were left on for the rest of the day just in case. And it was decided not to extubate her after all.

* * *

By then, minus the Tuesday before, she'd been intubated eight days. Much longer, we were told, and there was a good chance the damage to her vocal cords might be irreparable. She might never talk again. Also, having a foreign object like a breathing tube down the throat posed far more risk for infection than a trach, which was a third of the length if not less and whose inner cannula could be removed and disinfected. (I was almost as bad with trachs as I was with the heart. Single-lumen or double-lumen, fenestrated or non-fenestrated, cuffed or cuffless, Shiley or Bivona—I could never tell the differences or keep straight which or what size Mom had; it often changed depending on her progress weaning. All I knew was hers always consisted of at least two parts: the outer tube, its face plate sutured in place and additionally secured by an adjustable cloth neck strap, and that inner cannula, which slid and locked into the outer tube.)

It made perfect sense, and though I'd know better than to fall for the by-no-means-permanent/totally-normal-productive-lives spiel when used with regard to the G- and J-tubes, presently coming from the thoracic surgeon who'd end up performing the tracheos-tomy, I had no reason to doubt it. Still, things were moving way too fast. A little more than two weeks ago Mom had asked me to bring her some dental floss. Now she needed a hole cut into her throat.

The thoracic surgeon assured me that the result of the biopsy wouldn't make the trach any less necessary. Supposing the mass was found to be malignant, a PET scan—the most conclusive way to check for metastasis—couldn't be performed on someone who was intubated. (The breathing tube interferes with detection.) Just the same, wanting a little time to process everything, I asked if we could hold off on making any plans until the result came back.

That gave me all of six hours.

By the time we got to reSCU, near the first of the year, we had our schedule down. Claire would go up Monday through Saturday around ten o'clock and leave between two and three if it was a good day. If it was a bad one, she'd stay till I got there, around four thirty. Unless, as with the G- and J-tubes, there was a procedure scheduled in the morning—then I'd go up for the whole day and Claire would stay home. I'd stay till half past midnight or so, after Mom had received her Ambien and fallen asleep. This included Sundays, when Dad would relieve Claire. Melanie would come up Saturday early afternoon for a few hours. Roger and Alice would come up either Saturday or Sunday for a couple hours in the late afternoon. Roger would also stop by before flying out of Cleveland on business trips. And when she was in town, Elaine would come up with me.

In G-53, though, especially those first couple weeks, we didn't co-ordinate, and often, particularly in the evenings, three or four of us would be there at once, sometimes all six. Almost always, whether Dad or Roger or Melanie, there was at least one other person besides me for a portion of the eight-to-nine visiting hour. Except for that Tuesday night. I was by myself when Dr. Martin, dressed in surgical whites, appeared in the doorway and motioned me out into the unit. I already knew it. I mean, I just knew.

"Jesus Christ," I said.

"Jesus *fucking* Christ," he said. Just like that, with the emphasis. I know it's strange that should've meant and continues to mean so much to me. And the thing is, I'm not sure I can even tell you why. It wasn't that it showed he really cared about Mom, that he was genuinely upset. It did, but it was more than that, and more than his abandoning the propriety expected of a doctor. I don't know. It was just such a human thing to say. It made me feel less alone.

He couldn't tell me much, other than it was called squamous cell and that it was most commonly associated with smokers; an oncologist, one Dr. Graham, would be stopping by before the week was out to go into greater detail and discuss treatment options. In the meantime, Dr. Martin advised going ahead with the trach. I gave my assent. As for telling Mom, we agreed it best to wait till she was sufficiently cognizant. That wouldn't be for another month.

CHAPTER SIX

I.

Dating wasn't the only reason I started dressing better once in New York. The city's most luxury department store was a client of the catering company, and after hundreds of hours passing phyllo-wrapped asparagus spears and limoncello martinis at trunk shows for Michael Kors, Donna Karan, and Vera Wang, I couldn't help but get into haute couture. This appreciation was put to good use when, a couple years removed from receiving my MFA and still without a publication of any species to speak of, I took a fashion internship at a bimonthly arts-and-culture glossy hoping to parlay it into a byline or two. After a couple months alphabetizing lookbooks and gofering sample dresses used in photo spreads, I was finally given the chance to write a few front-of-book pieces and was apparently proficient enough that the assignments kept coming after the internship ended. They were mainly profiles of up-and-coming designers. Just a few months before coming home I'd interviewed a Belgian-born, Parisian-based protégé of Vivienne Westwood whose "fondness for arabesque prints," I wrote, "melds with her affinity for light construction."

However, along with the hair, the basketball, the issues surrounding the divorce, so would resurface my disdain for foppishness. And though I'd stop short of busting out the butterfly collars—other than a pair of jeans Elaine would buy me and a winter coat from Dad, those few clothes I'd packed were the entirety of my wardrobe—when Dr. Graham first showed up to the X-Box in his Versace horn-rims it was all I could do not to scoff and shake my head. The white jacket didn't help. Nor what he had to say.

In a couple ways, the discovery of the cancer had been a relief. It absolved the guilt and regret I'd been feeling for scorning the step-down doctors' recommendation that Mom go home and get stronger before she had her bypass. (Sure, had she gone home she might've better withstood the bypass, but in the meantime maybe the cancer, continuing to go undiscovered, would've progressed to the point that the bypass was needless. If the cancer *had* been discovered before the bypass, maybe it could've been removed surgically. But then in the time it'd have taken for her to recover from that and get strong enough for the bypass, maybe she'd have had another heart attack.) It also, we'd thought, finally explained the nausea and vomiting. But no, Dr. Graham now said, the cancer had nothing to do with that. And as for treatment, at this point there wasn't much he could do. In an otherwise healthy person, he'd have just cut out the lung's upper right lobe, where the tumor was located. But she was too weak for surgery—chemo, too. The only option was radiation, but even that couldn't be considered until she was out of the ICU and stronger. *And* that depended on whether the cancer was confined to that one spot. One potential explanation for the nausea and vomiting, Dr. Graham offered, was metastasis to the brain. That didn't appear to be the case from a recent CT scan, but he wouldn't be certain until after a PET scan.

"So when the hell's that gonna happen?" I asked.

"Hopefully in the next few days," he said.

"Hopefully?" I said. "It damn well better."

In his forties, thin and tall, with close-cropped dark hair and a slight widow's peak, Dr. Graham would become my favorite doctor, the one both Mom and I trusted most. Though under as little obligation to keep tabs on her as Dr. Martin—after the two radiation sessions in January, his job was done until the follow-up scheduled for May; after the ten sessions in July, no need to see her till fall sometime—he'd stop by her room in reSCU every afternoon around five, coming all the way over from the T Building, clear across the hospital. He'd ask how she was feeling that day and what all she'd done and was good at reading her lips. If she was asleep, I'd join him in the hall and fill him in. If I'd stepped out to use the phone or restroom, he'd leave his card on the tray table with the time and a note jotted on the back.

4:45. You were sleeping. I will see you tomorrow.

In time, there'd be almost nothing I'd find more reassuring than Dr. Graham's calm, deliberate manner of speech. But after Dr. Martin's impassioned frankness, it came off aloof and uncaring. After he left, I considered asking Dr. Martin if there weren't any other oncologists we could use.

In the end, I decided not to. If he's this up on fashion, I thought, imagine how attuned he must be to innovations and advancements in his own field.

* * *

However put off I was by the sight of those seven silver embossed letters on Dr. Graham's frames, the knowledge that someone among northeastern Ohio's high-waisted-stonewashed-jeans-and-white-sneaker faithful had at least heard of the label did make me feel less removed from New York. And that wasn't the only reminder.

There were the hours at a time on my feet, only instead of passing trays of food, I stood rubbing Mom's forehead or spoon-feeding her ice chips. The latex gloves I'd wear to put balm on her lips—just as much a pain to get on as the ones I'd use when helping the kitchen prep. The homeless who eluded the Main Campus cops to panhandle or sack out in the various waiting areas. The astringent urine smell like . . . well, like pretty much everywhere in the city.

TV. While in the two step-down units, we'd gotten hooked on *Cash Cab,* the A&E network's trivia game show that takes place in a Manhattan taxi. There were back-to-back episodes from five to six. Then I'd change it to TBS for *Seinfeld* and—those nights the Cavs weren't playing and there was no pregame show—leave it there for *Friends.* About halfway through our time in the X-Box, A&E moved *Cash Cab* to earlier in the afternoon. Following *Oprah* then—which, as with the Cavs, I'd put on in the hopes her voice might churn up some halcyon memories, for every day since I was in junior high Mom would set the VCR timer to record the show and watch it first thing after getting home from work or the gym—I'd switch to TBS an hour earlier for back-to-back episodes of yet another New York–based sitcom, *The King of Queens.* That *really* put me back there, one of the establishing shots being of the antiques store right across the street from our apartment in Astoria. Set in nearby Long Island was

Everybody Loves Raymond, on from seven to eight. I'd always dogged the show, but Mom liked it and after a couple months I warmed to it. "I'm worried about you," Elaine said when I told her so. She wasn't joking, and, taking her concern to heart, from then on I'd switch—even in reSCU when Mom was sentient—from *Friends* to ABC for *Wheel of Fortune* and *Jeopardy!*

II.

Once she was in the X-Box, the G-53 nurses let us stay past visiting hours. At first I tried cozying up to them thinking they'd then take even better care of Mom. Quickly, though, my affection became sincere, for Brian especially. He was only a couple years older than me, mid-thirties at most—tall, lean, soft-spoken, with a shaved head and always a stolid look on his face. He played in a hard-edged alt-rock band that was fairly well-known on the local scene and occasionally opened for bigger bands that came through. He was a few years married and had a new baby. He'd been in the unit four or five years but was lately considering going through the training to become an anesthesiology nurse—less stress and better pay, he claimed.

They'd also allow us to take off the restraints and the boots, which were meant to prevent foot drop as well as the skin on her heels from breaking down. The first pair we tried—molded plastic with a sheepskin lining—Mom complained were too hot. Another, inflatable type she didn't care for, either. Not being more insistent that she wear them and instead putting pillows under her legs would be a costly mistake. It is, in fact, the one thing I fault myself for, the only matter—outside of my eventual behavior toward Elaine—I wish I'd handled differently. Once we'd gotten to reSCU, anyway, and I still let her get away with it. I cut myself a little slack in G-53, when there was less concern over her ever walking again than living to see another day.

To ward off new pneumonias and keep those she had from worsening, one thing the nurses were absolutely inflexible about was getting her into a chair every day—a beat-up old recliner shared between the two glassed-in X-Box rooms. In order to do that, they had to call lift team—pairs of guys whose only job was to go around the hospital lifting people out of bed and putting them back in. Mom wasn't much of a challenge, especially later on, but I saw plenty of patients who wouldn't have looked out of place on the Browns' offensive line; I still can't figure how the sheet wouldn't rip, how the guys managed to get those folks airborne in the first place. Especially the pair we always got, every time—a lanky black guy in his early thirties and a shorter, paunchy white guy in his fifties who had the same drying-out, miscreant look I remembered of the lifer Portage caddies. For how long it took them to come, you'd think they were the *only* team. Their quickest response time was forty-five minutes. Usually it'd take twice that long. So that, as soon as they got Mom in the chair, before they'd left the unit even, the nurses would be right back on the phone with the dispatcher.

Poor thing—she'd get so exhausted I'd end up pushing the chair right up next to the bed so she could lay her head on the mattress. It was less the physical strain, though, than the fact that she was put through it in the middle of the night. So it seemed to her.

Being in the unit so long, in that isolated room, she'd developed what the nurses called "ICU psychosis," a symptom of which was inversion of time. Sure enough, there'd be nights when seven P.M. would roll around and she'd all of a sudden be wide-eyed, watching the game and asking for ice chips or to be put in the chair, not realizing she'd already been up a few hours earlier. When I'd tell her so, she wouldn't care, wanted to again, and when I'd say it wasn't possible, that lift team had already gone home for the night, she'd just go ahead and make to get up on her own. The first time or two, I remonstrated and threatened to put the restraints back on but then realized it was easier to just help her up and swing her legs over the side of the bed and sit with her on the edge there, clutching her around the shoulders to keep her from falling. After a couple minutes of that, she'd ask to lie back down and be calm the rest of the night.

Ice chips were all she was allowed to eat. And one or two of the rotating staff doctors forbade even this, what with the risk of aspiration and her proneness to pneumonia. For nutrition, then, once that central line in her thigh became infected and had to be removed and the TPN stopped, they'd put in a feeding tube—or Corpak, as the nurses called it, after the manufacturer. However, they didn't advance it into the jejunum, wouldn't begin doing so until after the gastric emptying test. And so resulted episodes such as the one Claire notes for Saturday, December 2: *Walked in room. Nurse asked me to leave. Susie had tried to get out of bed but threw up all over. Nurse had to change her.*

No, the time shake-up wasn't hard and fast, and there'd be days too when she'd show life. Wouldn't be all that with it, granted— disorientation another symptom of the psychosis (November 19: *Asked me, "Where am I?" Told her she was in intensive care. Asked: "Why?"*)—but would at least be awake. More often, though, she'd be zonked, days and nights both. Sometimes it was the pneumonias and their effect on her blood pressure. (Whenever the pressure dipped too low, the monitor would alarm, and, as instructed by the nurses, we'd lightly shake her to consciousness. She'd drift back off a minute later, the alarm would sound once more, and we'd rouse her again. Over and over.) Otherwise it was her being unruly, endangering herself, so she was sedated. Fentanyl. That's what's indicated on a list one of the nurses wrote out that's paperclipped to Claire's journal:

Aldactone 25 mg (diuretic—gets rid of water)

Pepcid 20 mg (stomach)

Nystatin swish/swallow (yeast infection)

Nystatin powder (yeast infection)

Synthroid 50 mcg (thyroid)

Zosyn 3.375 gram (antibiotics)

Vancomycin 1 gram (antibiotics)

Zyprexa 5 mg under tongue (antidepressant)

Lopressor 12.5 mg (blood pressure)

Reglan 10 mg (stomach—increases motility, decreases nausea)

Fentanyl drip (anesthetic—for comfort)

Insulin drip (sugar control)

Heparin drip (for mitral valve)

* * *

I'd make an entry in the journal every now and then, for those rare days Claire stayed home, but didn't keep one of my own. It was hard enough going through everything in real time. To then at the end of the day do it all again—fuck that.

I did read, though—*a lot,* the most since the MFA program's book-a-week syllabi. After all that TV my brain craved the nourishment. Plus it gave me a sense of normalcy. Whenever I came home from Tampa or New York to visit, on those nights when I wasn't at the Valley bars with the guys, I'd be shut up in my room bingeing on books instead of beer, listening to the murmur from the TV in Mom's room.

Maybe the best indication of the effect everything had on me, on my mental state, is to compare the first book I read with the last. The first was that one I'd packed—*The World of Chance,* by late-nineteenth-century novelist, critic, and southeastern Ohio native William Dean Howells. The book had been mentioned that April in a *New York Times Book Review* essay about the paucity of novels from the early-twentieth century onward taking ambition for their central theme. "Young Man from the Provinces," the writer called them: "YMFTP arrives in the city with nothing except talent and dreams of greatness; adventure and misadventure ensue." The essay had caught my attention because for some time I'd been thinking of embarking on just such a project—a roman à clef about coming to the city, grad school, catering. The description of *Chance*—". . . an Ohioan who arrives in New York with an unpublished novel and half-acknowledged fantasies of a glittering career . . ."—made it seem essential research. Unfortunately, like all but a couple of How-ell's sixty-odd works, it was long out of print. After trolling Alibris and AbeBooks daily for a month or so, I finally found a water-stained, leather-flaking 1893 printing decommissioned by a public library in Tucson, Arizona.

> *The sun was gay on the senseless facades of the edifices, littered with signs of the traffic within, and hung with effigies and emblems of every conceit and color, from the cornice to the threshold, where the showcases crowded the passengers to the curbstones, and to the cellarways that overflowed the sidewalks with their wares.*

The last book I read was Jim Thompson's 1955 noir *After Dark, My Sweet,* about a deranged ex–prize fighter who falls for a boozy femme fatale, joins in her plot to kidnap the child of a wealthy family, and, when it gets botched, decides to sacrifice himself so she can escape.

> *And that was all I wanted now. Just to get it over with, to have the end come. Because it was bound to be bad; no good, no happiness could come out of this now, so the quicker it was over the better.*
>
> *I'd have ended it myself if I could have. But somehow I couldn't, and I guess it wasn't so strange that I couldn't. There's something inside every man that keeps him going long after he has any reason to.*

The titles I remember in between: *Brideshead Revisited* and *Scoop, Appointment in Samarra* (the Lantenengo Country Club was Portage to a T), O'Hara's three-novella collection *Sermons and Soda Water, The Moviegoer, Tender Is the Night, The Road.* That one had been a gift from Elaine for my birthday. The rest I got either from her and Dad and the rest of the family at Christmas or the main library downtown. Though I hadn't used it in five years, my account was still valid; all I needed was a new card.

One book I checked out was Joan Didion's *The Year of Magical Thinking*—checked it out, brought it home, dropped it on the kitchen counter, and left it there till returning it a few weeks later. I finally worked up the nerve when I got back to New York—*Magical Thinking* and, on a friend's suggestion, Philip Roth's *Patrimony*. But neither did anything for me. Only one book has—not a loss memoir but *Dispatches,* Michael Herr's account of covering the Vietnam War for *Esquire.*

> *... more than in other life you don't really know what you're doing most of the time, you're just behaving, and afterward you can make up any kind of bullshit you want to about it, say you felt good or bad, loved it or hated it, did this or that, the right thing or the wrong thing; still, what happened happened.*

> *And sometimes the only reason you didn't panic was that you didn't have the energy.*

> *It wasn't possible, just not possible, to have been where we'd been before and to be where we were now ...*

There was also the article in *The New York Times Magazine* of May 25, 2008, about Sergeant Shurvon Phillip, a twenty-seven-year-old marine reservist who in Iraq three years earlier had suffered a traumatic brain injury when his Humvee struck an antitank mine.

Worse than quadriplegic, able to move only his eyelids and eyebrows and flare his nostrils, he was nourished by tube feed and had a trach. His mother was his full-time caregiver, sleeping every night in a recliner next to his bed, a vent and suction machine close by. In an accompanying photo, Sgt. Phillip lay braced by a half dozen pillows the same way Mom always was and wore the foot-drop boots. He was from Cleveland.

III.

What gets most people is that I went through all this without any brothers and sisters. But hearing stories from the few others I know or have met who've gone through a parent's prolonged illness *with* siblings—the squabbling over every little decision, the resentment toward those not pulling their weight, the resentment *those* folks feel toward whoever's picking up their slack along with envy over not being able to more fully share in the parent-child bonding—makes me glad I'm an only child. And besides, I wasn't on my own.

Claire had five grandkids and a bunch of close girlfriends, knitted baptismal bibs for the church, and as a Eucharistic minister delivered the sacrament at hospice once or twice a week. In other words, she had a life. And yet, going by her journal, in the little over three months between Mom arriving at the Clinic and being transferred to reSCU, she missed only five mornings; in the eleven or so months that followed—not counting Sundays—just twenty-seven, the majority of those due to either driving conditions or a procedure taking place early and Mom wanting me there instead. And this was a woman who'd just turned seventy.

Melanie handled all the work stuff: submitted the doctor's letter needed to procure Mom's paid medical leave; was the first to bring up filing for permanent disability—without her I'm not sure we'd have ever thought about it—and got us all the necessary paperwork; brought Mom's checks for me to deposit; cleaned out her office, boxed everything up, and dropped it off at the house; informed me of the employee life-insurance policy and how to claim the balance of Mom's pension.

Roger was often traveling for business but let it be known that if at any point I felt the doctors were pushing me around or not showing me enough respect because of my age, or if it might prove more advantageous for me to remain in their good graces, he was willing to come in and raise hell, play the bad cop to my good. It was never necessary. In fact, I believe I was treated with *more* respect because of my age and the sympathy it engendered, and was less concerned about falling out of favor with the doctors than with Mom for showing insufficient ire. Still, it was nice to know he had my back.

On top of her emotional support—the little I'd allow her to provide—Elaine sent me my mail and deposited my checks. I didn't have a savings account let alone any actual savings, so I lived off Mom's disability. Food, gas, ten dollars a day for parking (unless you bought a ten-day, forty-dollar discount booklet, which Dad, Claire, Roger, and Melanie started doing after the first month at the Clinic but which I, ever recalcitrant to admit the probability of another week and a half, resisted till around month three). And there was my rent. Mom's condition was always so precarious, there was never a time when I felt confident she'd be alive long enough for Elaine to get a subletter in the apartment. Even if I had, I still wouldn't have allowed it. I wouldn't have wanted Elaine to have to adjust to a new roommate on top of all the strain she was already under. Plus I wouldn't have been able to accept the permanence that'd bring. Eight hundred dollars a month was well worth it to be able to say I still lived in New York. A couple days before the first of the month and whenever my credit-card bill came due, then, Dad would cut me a check from Mom's checkbook, and for her bills as well—the house's utilities, the car insurance, her cell phone. (We didn't dare cancel it after the fuss she kicked up over Dad discontinuing pest control's monthly spray around the house's perimeter.) I wouldn't even bother to open the bills. I just dropped them off at his place on my way up to the Clinic.

One afternoon he asked me to wait a second before I left, said he needed to talk to me about something.

"I went to the doctor today," he said. "I've just been feeling so run-down lately. You know, getting up at seven to deliver the mail, then nights driving up to the hospital and back. All the stress. The doctor says I should probably stop going up as much, so I think I am. I'm thinking just one night a week from now on."

Then he broke into tears. I went over to where he was standing by the kitchen sink and put my hands on his shoulders.

"I just don't want to let you down," he said.

I put my arms around him. He put his around me.

"You're not," I said. "You only would if you wound up making yourself sick. I can't be worrying about the both of you."

"Are you sure?"

"Swear. I'm glad you said something."

We hugged for a minute more. I went to the bathroom and got him some toilet paper to blow his nose.

"I'm thinking Thursdays," he said. "Unless another night would be better."

"Thursdays should work," I said. (It wasn't till we got to reSCU that it occurred to me to have him come Sundays and give Claire a break. And I'd been the one to suggest it, not her.)

"I mean, if you ever do need me up there, I'm there. I mean it. I don't want you to think you can't ask me."

"I know. And if I do, I will. Promise."

As I left, he reminded me to call as soon as I could to let him know how Mom took the news. That night—Wednesday, December 13—Dr. Martin planned to tell her about the biopsy, the cancer.

I know I said we waited till she was sufficiently cognizant, but was she really? After referencing the journal, I'm not so sure. *She was alert & knew me,* Claire wrote of that morning, and for that to be noteworthy . . . Brian and the rest of the regular G-53 staff knew not to say anything, but there were plenty of floaters who came through—nurses who filled in for whatever unit was in most need—so maybe the decision to tell her was made out of a growing worry that one of them might let it slip. If she was going to hear it, better that it be from Dr. Martin.

He stood on the side of the bed nearest the door. I was on the other. She didn't take it hard at all. She didn't cry, and after he'd finished, all she asked was if she could have some ice cream. Strawberry, I remember—remember thinking after Dr. Martin gave his permission, "That's not going to be pretty coming back up." Which, of course, it did, and it wasn't.

That was the reason for her reaction—or lack thereof. "Now I know why I've been throwing up," she mouthed between bites. I didn't disabuse her. Who knew? Maybe that was just the thing she needed, to think there was a light at the end of the tunnel—a really long fucking tunnel, but still a glimmer down there.

Considering she'd be transferred to reSCU just over two weeks later, it'd seem that's precisely how it happened—that once she got word of the cancer, there occurred an immediate turnaround in her condition, as if she'd willed it. But while I don't discount a change in her attitude helping things, in reality it wasn't till two days before the transfer that the possibility was even mentioned. The day before *that* was Christmas, and she'd been out of it like always.

We did our best to get her in the spirit—as well as give her a better sense of the time of year. Claire brought in a tiny fake tree with lights and set it where Mom could see, on the small supply chest by the window. A few Christmas cards had come to the house—some from old friends unaware of what had happened, including one of the Social Security girls who mentioned needing to set a date for their annual dinner. These I taped to the wall along with the dozens of other get-well cards and the orange poster board Claire had covered with photos already hanging there. I bought a red throw blanket from Target and wrapped it, took one of her hands and ran it over the paper, then stripped it off myself and draped the blanket over her.

I'd come up early. Claire stayed home to finish getting dinner ready. Dad had agreed to come in the late afternoon so I could spend the rest of the night at Claire's, with the family. That's what Mom would want, I told myself.

Since moving to the X-Box, she'd banned anyone from visiting except the six of us and Elaine—a ban she'd uphold for the duration. One night Sully dropped by unannounced, and though he swore he wouldn't stay, only wanted to say hi and give her his love, she refused to let him in the room. She didn't want anyone seeing her in the state she was. And visitors tired her out. Once in reSCU, she needed to save the energy for weaning.

The cousins and their spouses and kids were all full of questions. It pissed me off—a horrible thing to say, but it did. I'd hoped to forget everything for the night. After I didn't give them much in the way of responses, they got the message and quit asking. But to have her not be talked about at all pissed me off even more. I was a fucking mess, likely suffering from a bit of ICU psychosis myself, uncomfortable with normal human interaction outside the hospital, unable to comprehend how all of us could be right where we were every year, doing the same things we always did—Jeff carving the turkey, Claire saying grace—and Mom fifty miles away. Just fifty stupid miles. It wasn't worse than if she'd been dead, I'd realize the following Christmas, but at the time it sure felt like it.

"Kind of figured I might see you again," Dad said when a couple hours later I walked back into the room. We stood to either side of the bed watching the twenty-four-hour *Christmas Story* marathon while taking turns rubbing her head.

CHAPTER SEVEN

I.

The year I asked for a bike, they pulled a *Christmas Story* and, after I'd opened all my presents and began to pout, sent me to grab something from the rec room where, set up on its kickstand, there was a BMX and beside it the camcorder to capture me collapsing to my knees in a fit of girlish squealing. That next year, after I'd left the bike in the garage to rust and turned to skateboarding, they had built a five-foot quarter pipe. I got Nintendo the first Christmas it came out, the first Upper Deck complete set. I even made out at Easter, when they'd hide plastic eggs with clues inside leading me all over the house and ultimately to my basket, overflowing with chocolate and always containing one big-ticket item, such as the Swatch when I was nine. I eventually got those baserunning-only batting gloves, too.

No, I never rued being an only child, especially since our extended family was so tight and I was so close to my cousins, all of whom doted on and roughhoused with me no differently than if I'd been their little brother. As for Mom, Dad says she'd wanted more kids. But then she might not have had any more even if she hadn't gotten sick. Not with Dad, anyhow.

* * *

They'd been separated a year and a half. He'd taken his own apartment. Then she got sick and he moved back home. Though aware of his absence, I was too young to be affected by it. In fact, so much did I take their situation for granted, so natural did I assume it, that when they finally divorced, I failed to make the correlation to the separation, never thought, Well, it wasn't like there wasn't precedent. Actually, it was even more surprising *because* of the separation.

See, by that summer between eighth and ninth grade, I'd become the most hopeless of romantics. This might seem odd given my then adoration for a musical genre typically associated with the objectification and debasement of women, one whose videos featured ten-foot-tall plaster asses and poor girls unable to play a game of backyard volleyball without being deprived of their bikini tops. However, at that time in hip-hop, just as there were acts who averted that censorious black-and-white brand, there were those who espoused a more genteel prurience—Mary J. Blige looking for real love, Heavy D wondering what to do with it once he'd found it. I won't deny rhyming along with the rest of the class to "Baby Got Back" on the bus ride to Washington, D.C., for our eighth-grade trip—that cassingle was all we played, over and over, until the boombox's batteries ran out—but at home in the shower would just as soon spit Eric B. and Rakim's "What's on Your Mind?" or the Pharcyde's "Passin' Me By." When, that is, I wasn't practicing Continentals songs.

It's hard to believe, given how rough-and-tumble Litchfield was. To be fair, it was probably the safest middle school in the district, but even so, not a week went by without a fight. I'm talking real brawls. Guys trading punches, smashing one another into lockers and the cafeteria's wall of windows. The girls were even more vicious. In what had to be the nastiest altercation during my two years there, this chick got beat so bad in the hall between classes she pissed herself—left a puddle on the floor and everything. Quarters were always being pitched or craps shot in the bathroom. A couple kids already had kids and one had been held back so many times he drove himself to school. And yet somehow the pinnacle of popularity— even more so than sporting the latest Merry-Go-Round ensemble— was belonging to the eighth grade's audition-only female and male retro-fifties vocal groups, the Doo-Wops and Continentals.

We wore leather jackets over white tees, the ladies letterman sweaters and poodle skirts. Our repertoires consisted of golden oldies such as "Rockin' Robin" and "Leader of the Pack" and came accompanied by intricately choreographed dance steps and hand jives. The reason everyone wanted to do it was because it got you out of class a few times a semester. We performed at King and other elementary schools and at functions hosted by the Rotary Club and Women's League. Our biggest audience was at the winter choral and band recital, held for parents and family on a mid-December school night in the gymnasium. While we were onstage that evening, the girls sat on the risers with their chins cupped in their hands staring up at us all moony-eyed and fake whispering about our dreaminess just as we would for them. It was all part of the act. And yet—for me, at least—it was hard not to get swept up in it, to not feel like I'd been transported back to a more chaste era.

The feeling didn't dissipate once the recital ended; as was Doo-Wop and Continental tradition, we went to G.D. Ritzy's, a faux-fifties diner in the Valley with vinyl booths, college pennants on the walls, nickel-a-play tabletop jukeboxes, and soda jerks in white paper hats. Nor did it once we'd finished our chili dogs and chocolate malteds and gone home . . . nor the next day . . . nor the next *week*. Difficult though it was to fathom Main Street having ever been anything other than a ghost town, that Crosby area a ghetto, those tire factories rubble, the rest of Akron and its surrounding environs— excepting Tan 'N' Yogurt and Summit Mall—were stuck in the very same postwar, *American Graffiti* time warp.

There were not one, not two, but *three* lights-for-service drive-ins— my favorite, Swenson's, established in 1934 on the very same plot of land where it continues to reside. Also in that business district known as Wallhaven was a McDonald's with the original single-arch sign; one of the first ever Arby's, *its* sign a fifty-foot-tall ten-gallon hat illuminated by hundreds of lightbulbs; and another Krispy Kreme, not quite so old as the Maple Street location (est. 1939) but with a similarly passé neon marquee.

Nearer to downtown was the Art Deco Diamond Grille steak house (est. 1934), to whose chrome-stooled bar Grandpa Manning had not infrequently bellied up, as would the pros when in town for whatever the Firestone tournament was calling itself that year; Luigi's (est. 1949), where Sully had worked, its walls covered with autographed black-and-white head shots of Lou Monte, the Harmonicats, and other yesteryear performers who'd once passed through; Mary Coyle Ice Cream Parlor (est. 1937), like Ritzy's bedecked with pennants as well as Tiffany lamps, collectible candy tins, and other vintage bric-a-brac. Over on the east side was another purveyor of homemade ice cream, Strickland's (est. 1936), whose walk-up window on summer nights always stretched twenty people long.

A stone's throw from Strickland's was Derby Downs—easily Akron's most famous hill. Since 1937, it'd been home to the All-American Soap Box Derby, the amateur youth sport's world championship and to this day one of Americana's most enduring exemplars—not only the competition but also the week's worth of festivities preceding it: the parades, ceremonies, appearances by stars of sport and screen. That's about the only thing that *has* changed in seventy-odd years, the pedigree of the celebrities. Jimmy Stewart attended consecutive derbies in the late forties—blowing off, on one occasion, a string of Broadway performances and, on another, his honeymoon. The summer I moved to New York the best the organizers could do was Dennis Haskins, *Saved by the Bell*'s Principal Belding.

Speaking of, there was the *SBTB* episode in which Zach and the gang form a doo-wop group of their own. *Beverly Hills, 90210* with its pompadours, Dylan McKay's Porsche, the Ritzy's-like Peach Pit; *The Wonder Years*. The movies of my youth were even more steeped in nostalgia: *A Christmas Story, Hoosiers, The Natural, La Bamba, Stand by Me, Dead Poets Society, School Ties, Cry Baby, Edward Scissorhands, Peggy Sue Got Married, Eddie and the Cruisers, The Heavenly Kid*, the *Little Shop of Horrors* remake, anything with Diane Lane, the cars in *Christine* and *Ford Fairlane*, and of course *Back to the Future*. I now understand that the real reason I loved that film so much, ahead of the DeLorean's doors and the skateboarding scenes, was my ability to relate to Marty McFly's feelings of displacement.

All this—plus Magic 105.7, Cleveland's oldies station, preset on both Mom's and Dad's car radios—fueled my romanticism, supplied the idyllic lens through which, by the time of the divorce, I'd come to view my life, Mom and Dad's relationship above all else. Theirs was a love of the sort that inspired those three-part harmonies our puberty-warped voices mercilessly butchered, a love as epic as that of Roy and Iris, Ritchie and Donna, Dylan and Brenda, Dylan and Kelly, Brandon and Kelly—and the separation, her sickness, and what I perceived as his coming to the rescue only made it more so. After all that, how could they not be meant to be together forever?

II.

More than for its dress code I chose Walsh—despite my cousins' threats of excommunication from the family—because that's where Ben and most of my Litchfield buddies were going. They all played freshman football, though—I didn't last much longer at Pee Wee than Dad had walking on at U of A—so for a time we drifted apart. And I lost touch with the middle school gang attending Firestone High. Those were a hard few months between Dad leaving and my befriending Sully, the only time I'd ever wished for a brother or sister. But aside from its poor timing, unique as the divorce was— incomparable, I'd go so far as to say, judging from any other kids of divorce I've ever known—I couldn't have come through it any less unscathed. After all, so little changed.

She sent him a card and some instant lottery tickets for his birthday. He brought flowers to the house on hers. He came over Christmas morning and we opened presents together. They'd get each other one or two and most of the tags on mine would read FROM MOM AND DAD. Later in the day, he'd stop by Claire and Max's for dinner. They took me out for my birthday, and a lot of times when he'd come over after work to play catch in the street like always—him uphill, to increase my arm strength as well as keep him from chasing after my overthrows—she'd set him a place at the table. They sat together at my basketball and baseball games, at that National Honor Society ceremony. They were both there while I test-drove my first car, both dickered with the dealer over the price. They moved me into my dorm in Tampa and were back four years later sitting next to each other watching me receive my diploma. They sat next to each other watching Sully receive his. Whenever I flew in from Tampa or New York, they'd pick me up at Akron-Canton and we'd go straight to Swenson's.

Forget other kids of divorce—I've known plenty whose parents were married and not half as close. For a good long while, until I'd experienced enough of love to begin to appreciate how very different it is from compatibility, this was more confusing than if the split had been acrimonious: if, say, they'd bad-mouthed each other to me. More confusing but not more difficult, I knew even then—knew how lucky I was.

The split was even more endurable since it didn't come with the usual shift in parental roles. Take discipline.

Toward strangers Dad has never had difficulty expressing his anger. After a JV game in which I'd come off the bench to score three straight buckets only to be promptly and inexplicably sat the rest of the night, he got into a shouting match with the coach and had to be dragged away by Mom and one of the other fathers. Once when walking through a parking lot he noticed a man in one of the cars beating on his female companion, presented himself as an off-duty cop, and asked if the woman wished to press charges. (Fortunately for his sake—if not her own—she didn't.) And there was the Sunday night in reSCU when he felt Mom's abdominal pain was dismissed too out of hand by the staff doctor and went off on an invective-laced tirade reminiscent of those he so often witnessed growing up.

For precisely that reason, however, toward me he always kept the lid on. Mom would often and with no shortage of affection tell the story of how when I was five or six he tried to spank me and wound up crying more than I did. Only two or three times can I ever remember him raising his voice—and that's counting the argument we got into shortly after she died. Reaming me out, banishing me to my room—that had always fallen to Mom anyway. At the same time, for my more serious offenses, she continued to confer with him on punishment. In the attempted hoop-theft incident, my friend and I would ultimately evade those dogged flatfeet; but when, overcome with guilt, I confessed to Mom, she in turn consulted Dad, and rather than commend me for my honesty, he contacted the hoop's owner and indentured me to a couple afternoons of landscaping.

Perhaps her dealing with me on the subject of sex was one of those role shifts, but it probably would have been that way even if they'd stayed together. Dad wasn't any more comfortable explicating heavy breathing than he was with being the heavy. Our "talk" lasted all of five minutes, wherein he proselytized its sanctity, the spiritual as much as physical fulfillment to be derived from it, yet never bothered to define this "it" to which he was referring. Plus it was part of

Mom's job. When not doing home visits, she was in the neonatal clinic, often seeing girls my age. Junior year she brought home half a dozen condoms and put them in one of the drawers to Grandpa Hesidence's old desk. "I'm not giving you permission," she said. "But if you're going to anyway, be smart about it." Throughout high school there was hanging from the neck of the showerhead a plastic do-not-disturb-type sign with illustrations showing how to check for testicular cancer.

After I left for Tampa she moved to the clinic full-time. On top of the neonatal duties, administering travel vaccines, and screening for tuberculosis, she conducted STD exams and tested for HIV. "Sean, the amount of warts on this poor guy . . ." or "I'd never seen the color this ooze was . . ." She wasn't trying to scare me—well, maybe a little. But more so she was just enthralled by the job, endlessly fascinated by it, and it made me so happy to see her like that, I never stopped her.

Of course, it did scare me—enough that I wouldn't lose my virginity till twenty-one. Then, just when I'd mastered my neuroses, I was told by a recent ex there was a chance she might've given me chlamydia. Without insurance, I paid a visit to Manhattan's free clinic.

"I have a whole new respect for what you do," I told Mom after the results had come back negative.

"You should be using one for that, too," she said. "On her and you."

"Her?"

"Just take a pair of scissors, cut it, and stretch it over. That or use some Saran Wrap."

"Mom!"

"That swab felt good, did it?"

How many men had locked eyes on my high school graduation photo there on the shelf in her office to keep from passing out in pain while she shoved a Q-tip up their urethra? I know of at least one—a friend who after her death confided that Mom had once examined him. It was neither his first nor last trip to the clinic. Of all the nurses who'd seen him, she was the best, he said.

III.

It's surprising given Mom's support of contraception and defense of divorce—both she and Dad found the idea of annulment repugnant, were proud of the marriage, didn't want it expunged—what a devout Catholic she was, especially later in life. That's another thing that makes me wonder if she anticipated some calamity.

If in her twenties she was less at odds with the church than Dad over all that sin and guilt the nuns had literally pounded into them day after day for a dozen years—why he was so attracted to self-help's message of affirmation—it wasn't by much. "I can't remember what grade it was," he says. "But one time she was making confession and the priest started admonishing her and she told him, 'You have no right to say that about me,' and walked out."

She started warming to Catholicism after I was born—whatever their own issues, they both felt it important I be baptized and raised in the faith till I was old enough to make up my own mind, through confirmation at least—but it was with getting sick, being faced with her own mortality, that she fully embraced it. *That,* I'm sure she'd say, before nursing even, was the real windfall from the Hodgkin's.

All the same, just as with being a cancer survivor, she wasn't showy about her spirituality. No crucifix necklaces. A palm frond stuck in her car visor but no ichthys on the bumper. Except for a cross in each of our rooms, no iconography in the house. So at the time I just figured the pilgrimages she took with Claire those last couple years to Fátima and New Mexico's El Santuario de Chimayo were more about bonding with her sister and seeing someplace new. Now . . .

"No," Claire said when I asked about Mom's prescience. "I don't think that. Not at all."

"I don't know about the religion aspect," Dad said. "But absolutely she knew something was coming."

He reminded me of the insurance papers he found in the Corolla's glove box when cleaning it out to sell—the rider that paid off the rest of the bank loan in the event of disability or death, one few people take out due to the high premium. When I mentioned her changing the power of attorney, however, he said, "You've got that wrong. That was only after she'd gotten sick. I can remember signing the papers in the hospital." I swore it was before then, but Claire still has a copy, dated the day before the bypass. So it must've been Mom herself who'd stressed that the decision to divide the power of attorney wasn't any reflection on me. But then what of all that ready-to-put-the-marriage-behind-her business? Had she not been after all?

The most hopeless of romantics.

CHAPTER EIGHT

I.

G-81 spanned roughly half of Ninety-sixth Street from the corner of Carnegie toward Euclid—maybe three quarters of a football field in length. Thirty of its thirty-six rooms were devoted to either pulmonary or ear, nose, and throat inpatients, generally two per room. The other six, at the Euclid end, were for those weaning off ventilators. This was reSCU. Because the vents were so large—think a refrigerator minus the freezer—the rooms were all single occupancy. Between what Claire listed in the journal and the envelopes to the cards people sent—she moved around so much that January that on one envelope there'd been written and crossed out three rooms/units before it finally reached her—I count us in four of the six, though to see one was to have seen them all: two armchairs (one high-backed, one low); the tray table where Dr. Graham would drop his cards, its dark wood veneer matching that of the small chest near the foot of the bed in whose drawers were kept alcohol wipes, rolls of tape and gauze, trach-care kits, scissors, tweezers, clamps, and other supplies; a half bath into whose toilet nurses and aides dispatched the contents of urine foleys, bed and vomit pans, fecal and chest and G-tubes;

one wall a picture window, the others cream colored; suspended
TV; wall clock; assignment board; weekly mouth-care calendar
stocked with swabs corresponding to each shift; wall suction unit
with clear plastic canister for collecting secretions; and vent, always
to the side of the bed closest to the door and, in the event of an emergency, the in-rushing RT.

In each room we added a few personal touches: the poster board
of photos, which were transferred to a corkboard when the tape finally lost its stick; a white ceramic lamp I'd also picked up at Target
after the brightness of the overheads finally proved too unbearable; a
small oscillating fan to mask the hallway noise as much as to keep
her cool; a plush duck and a baby chick that quacked when its belly
was pressed—these an Easter present from Claire; also courtesy of
Claire, a small silver crucifix kept on the window ledge alongside
the materials for cleaning her—the bundles of diapers and under-
pads (or "chucks"), packets of disposable wipes, tubes of Xenaderm
and other ointments and creams.

Except for these flourishes, though, the only discrepancy between
reSCU's rooms was the direction the beds faced—and in Mom's case,
that hers was the near full-sized inflatable rather than the standard
twin (easier on the backside, less conducive to skin breakdown). Even
the views were similar in their obstruction: on the western-facing side,
the Terminal Tower and rest of downtown blotted by the looming
steel skeleton of the new heart center (ground for which was broken
one year to the day before Mom's heart attack), while to the east, the
wooded hills of suburban Cleveland Heights by the InterContinental—
close enough to see the guests milling about in their suites.

*   *   *

It was thought the change of scenery would take care of the ICU psychosis. Instead it worsened. December 31: *Told me she wanted me to take her to my house for 2 hrs! Told her I would love to but she had all those wires connected.* These—her IVs, the vent hose, the Corpak—she continued to pick and yank at, plus she still kept trying to get out of bed. Looking to create a peaceful atmosphere, however, one that wouldn't add to the anxiety brought on by weaning, reSCU didn't use restraints. They sat an aide in the room to keep watch. This made Mom even more agitated, so the doctors agreed to move the aide just outside the door as long as a family member was present. That's when I started staying so late.

The exacerbation of the psychosis was the result of a change in meds, a reaction to the Ativan they'd started giving her when she arrived in reSCU. Once that was discontinued and replaced by Xanax she calmed down, became more lucid and started getting back to her old self—was even playing crazy eights with Claire and tic-tac-toe with me. In that spiral notebook Claire first brought to H-22, which from then on we kept handy for when Mom wanted to write, are a bunch of grids and Xs and Os.

When she was healthy, Mom's handwriting was magnificent. "That's the one thing I gotta give parochial school," she'd say—her majestic uppercase Y with its great looping tail evoking sheaves of parchment and feathered quills. And constant—the script in a letter she gave me before heading off to Tampa identical to that of the birthday card that would sit on the steps of our apartment those first eleven days till Elaine got back, there in the box among the confetti and gone-stale brownies. So to see what became of it in that notebook might be the saddest thing of all. It's never the same twice. On one page the letters take up three or four lines, the next not even half of one. Every now and then there's an inkling of what it'd once been—a flawless capital *S* or lowercase *r*—but mostly it's the shaky, tentative cursive of a third-grader just learning. Or often just squiggly print. Or an erratic mixture of the two—here angled forward, there back.

Blood clot in right arm no massage only back rub

How's the weather?

Lift team waited 2 hrs today

Wine—1–2 glasses on weekend

Not a breakfast eater lunch and dinner more

Lightheaded

Lose all track of time

I wonder how she decorated the house?

It's not your fault

Right arm pain last night took Tylenol better

Lasix

Versed

Reglan

Zyprexa

Something for anxiety

How often can you take Xanax

Xanax helps

No Ativan

Didn't feel like hallucinations

Didn't sleep well

Slept good

I've always had trouble sleeping

They have no plan?

Older Dr.—We'll get you back on track

Hope it works

Help me with writing

In the Valley?

BP 88/55

Clinton runs for Pres

Legs swollen and stiff

I am having some problems memory

I missed Xmas totally

I move slow so please be patient

The tall one said, "You want me to wash your feet?"

I'm scared and confused don't know what's going on!

Hopeful!

Discouraged

Burping

Nauseated

Vomit

Sneezing then vomit

Nerves

Hard to give up control

Gas

No BM since yesterday

Can I keep bedpan at bed + try + go myself

New fecal bag?

That was a great vacation

Waves

I love her coming here she helps a lot

Tell me about it I just wish we could <u>talk</u>

I think what you did was okay

What is it like outside?

I what?

Do you believe I've been here 4 mo.

Why do I hurt so bad

Overdid it yesterday

Monday and Tuesday felt really good

Ice cream?

Orange popsicle

Peaches

Soup

Mac + che

Ketchup

Chocolate pudding

Ice chips

Not allowed to eat

I need to be pulled up so I can eat

Too salty

Don't feel hungry

2 units blood he said it would $\uparrow$ O2 to heart

Test tomorrow

Radiation @ 9

I had a CAT couple days ago

So if you take out line you would replace?

Regis Live

Deal or No Deal last night

What's on tonight? Dancing?

Everything was going okay then this

Give me reassurance!

Could you give me a backrub

Thirsty

Thank you

Sorry!

Go Buckeyes!

Blood in suction tube

Ambu bag

Greg when did he give me a

II.

The respiratory therapists all had different approaches. Wendy, for instance. I suspect I might've misjudged her, and that all her talking was—an approach, a tactic. That she meant for it to be diversionary, and that outside of reSCU she was quiet, introverted. Like Andre, only in reverse. I'd later run into him at Fairview, where he moonlighted. He was affable and smiling, so happy to learn we'd moved, asking for our room number so he could come by and say hi, nothing like the guy I'd known in reSCU—unemotive, no small talk, not so much as a glance at the TV, coming in to suction or attach or remove a breathing treatment then getting out. Not curt, just efficient, all business. Wouldn't put her back on full support before the staff doctor had ordered unless absolutely warranted by the numbers.

Not like Louise, who didn't put a whole lot of stock in the numbers, knowing how little they could be trusted. She was more concerned with how Mom looked, how hard she seemed to be working, how rapidly her chest rose and fell. If Mom insisted on being put back on, Louise rarely hesitated. "I always try to put myself in their place," she once told me. "I just can't imagine how terrifying it must be."

Kevin would haggle. Say the order called for Mom to stay off the vent till ten and she was asking to go back on at seven—he'd say nine, she'd come back with eight, and they'd meet in the middle at eight thirty. (And better believe at eight twenty-five she was hitting the call button. Eight thirty meant back on at eight thirty, not Kevin just then lumbering into the room. She was a stickler like that with all the RTs, each of whom had at least once caught daggers for making her wait.)

I absolutely got Kevin wrong. He was late forties, early fifties. Big—six two, six three—with floppy brown hair parted down the middle, probably the same since high school. I always took him for a goof—the way when working the ambu bag in between suctioning to help Mom catch her breath he'd rest his other elbow on the bed's top guardrail and complain about the Indians, especially starting pitcher Cliff Lee, who would rebound the following year to win the Cy Young Award but had such a lousy 2007 season he was eventually demoted to the minors. He didn't appear invested the way Greg or Nurse Stephanie or Dr. Graham were, certainly didn't bring the job home the way they seemed to. It wasn't until walking in on him holding Mom on her side while the doctor placed that central line in her neck that I realized my mistake. After they'd finished and I went back into the room, the first thing she mouthed was, and with her face still wet from the tears: "Kevin held my hand." Of all the incredible acts of kindness shown to her in those months, that's the one that sticks with me the most.

Theresa who was pregnant and worked the midnight shift; the older Asian guy whose gift for gab surpassed even Wendy's; the goateed guy a little older than me who explained how he never went to movies anymore, just got them on his computer through file sharing. Every RT had his or her own unique way, and there was something to be said for each. Honestly, I can't knock any of them. Never mind the cutting-edge gadgetry and unconventional weaning protocols— the respiratory therapists made reSCU what it was. They *were* reSCU—the nurses and aides too, but especially the RTs. If Mom had to choose one, though, it'd have been Greg.

Like Kevin, he was in his late forties or early fifties, trim, medium height, with salt-and-pepper hair, a thick, well-manicured mustache, and metal-framed glasses. He averaged sixty hours a week easy—rare was the day he wasn't working a double. I forget where he lived but it was no quick commute and had a long driveway that was troublesome in the snow. He had a teenage son, a baseball player and model kid from the sound of it but a teenager nonetheless. And yet the strain was never evident. He always came promptly when every five minutes she'd ask the nurse to get him; never showed exasperation at her pleading to be put back on; always gave the same lulling, soft-voiced encouragement. *You're doing fantastic. You really are. I know . . . I know it's hard. But you're doing awesome. I'm telling you. You should be really proud of yourself. You can do it. I know you can.* When she was in the high-backed chair and too exhausted to simply hold her head up, he'd go to one knee so he could look her in the eye.

That first week, his or any pep talks were unnecessary. She weaned fast, was soon on the trach collar (a small oxygen mask fitting over the trach and kept in place by an elastic neckband), getting into the chair, remaining there up to three hours at a time, and with the help of the nurses even walking to the door and back. She was able to go with just an oxygen tank to her first radiation session.

Whether the radiation wiped her out or her lungs were just fatigued or a combination of both, a couple days after that first session she had to be put back on full support. Then her blood pressure dropped, and as a precaution—reSCU, for all its sophisticated monitoring, being without the telemetry to track blood pressure, leaving the nurses to obtain it manually—she was sent to the sixth-floor ICU, where she'd spend the next few days. Soon she was in good enough shape to go from the ICU to her second radiation session—this time, as would be the case in July, with a portable vent and an accompanying RT—and that same night returned to reSCU. But with her being pumped full of fluids from the ICU, the weaning was slow going when it was going at all.

Heart, cancer, stomach, vent. Any one of these would've been near impossible to overcome, let alone all four. The heart, stomach, and vent conspired to take surgery and chemo off the table, while the location of the tumor and the constant vomiting made weaning even more of a struggle than it already was thanks to her ejection fraction (only slightly improved from the bypass). There was the suggestion, presented by more than one doctor, that the gastroparesis might lessen with increased activity, but again the other three ailments saw to it that *that* didn't happen.

The blood-pressure conundrum, though, posed the biggest challenge to her recovery. It was constantly low, almost always in the eighty-over-fifty range, teetering on the brink between acceptable hypotension and shock. Fluid raised it but, as in G-53 early on, would then just sit on her, causing even more severe edema than I'd seen in General—January 19: *Hands too puffy to feed herself so I fed her*—and compressing her lungs, making it a chore to breathe even on full support. Lasix was again used to draw it off, but a tad too much and her pressure once again dropped and back she went to the ICU—how she wound up again on the sixth floor just two weeks after leaving. Only this time things were much more serious, as she was found to be septic from some infected line or other. She'd rebound, be back in reSCU three days later, but that's when her case manager stepped in and *long-term care* first entered my vocabulary.

General, the Clinic, Fairview, *Grey's Anatomy*'s Seattle Grace—what we commonly know as hospitals are considered short-term acute care. The maximum stay is about ten days. If by then you're still not up to going home or to an inpatient rehabilitation facility but are stable enough to be out of intensive care, you may, depending on the optimism of your prognosis, be eligible for a long-term acute-care facility, or LTAC. An LTAC offers vent weaning; physical, speech, and occupational therapy; nutrition management including the accommodation of tube feeding—essentially, all the same services as reSCU. Actually, I failed to see any difference between the two— one reason I was so opposed to the move.

ReSCU had been active since 1993, its staff doctors helping the Clinic to a seventh-place *U.S. News* ranking in pulmonology for 2006. No LTAC could compete with that experience and expertise, and certainly not with the excellence of reSCU's staff, with whom there was the added advantage of their knowing Mom, liking her, appreciating all she'd been through, and having developed a personal stake in her success, always putting forth the extra effort. After wiping down her back when cleaning her, for instance, the aides would apply the moisturizer I'd brought in. (The Clinic moisturizer was too greasy.) Or if she'd already cleaned the unit out of Diet Sierra Mist, the nurses would go check for some in G-80 or another floor even. Little things, but everything to Mom. In an LTAC, she'd be just another fresh admit. She'd have to ingratiate herself from scratch, and without much time to do it.

"Long-term" means about a month. At the end of that period, if you still haven't been discharged, one of two things can happen. The doctors, feeling suitable progress has been made and that it's only a matter of time before you're home or in rehab, permit you to stay (provided the insurance company consents). Or they deem your improvement insufficient, project recovery as unlikely, and send you packing to a skilled nursing facility (which, don't be fooled, is just a less scary name for nursing home). There or to hospice.

When compared with ten days, a month seems a reasonable amount of time to assess a patient's chances. But hardly for someone in Mom's circumstances. Just into her fifth month of hospitalization, it was ridiculous to expect enough of an about-face in only four weeks to satisfy LTAC doctors. Especially now that she was back on full support, once again waterlogged from the ICU, still getting over the sepsis.

This, the case manager claimed, was the reason for her ingression and eagerness to see Mom go: So long as she stayed in the Clinic, she'd just keep winding up in intensive care with infection after infection until one finally did her in. And yet how would that risk be reduced in an LTAC?

The two LTACs I managed to get to before the issue was dropped were housed within short-term acute-care hospitals—General and Akron's other major hospital, Summa. Owned and operated by a separate company, they simply rented space; while relying on their landlords for certain services—such as at Grace when Mom's Corpak needed replacing or the final scan—the LTACs were self-contained, with their own staff and equipment and storehouse of meds. Still, were they not in hospitals the same as reSCU was in the Clinic?

In fact, at first glance those two LTACs seemed to pose more risk for infection than reSCU. At Summa's, more critical cases like Mom were all kept in the same small room, the half dozen or so beds facing one another. General's appeared more sanitary, the rooms all private, but, separate housekeeping or no, I couldn't shake the image of that funky pile of linens in the third-floor ICU waiting area—*still* there for all I knew.

Even if the risk had been less—and it wasn't, Mom coming down with both a UTI and *C. difficile* (or "C. diff," a bacterial infection common in hospitals that results in severe diarrhea and, in more serious cases, can lead to bowel perforation, kidney failure, and other life-threatening conditions) at Grace—there was still the hallway plaque to account for. It'd been presented by the family of a former patient to commemorate the reSCU staff's dedication and tireless determination during the *eleven months* it'd taken their loved one to wean. What about that person? Where'd been the concern over infection for them?

What it was really about, I figured, was money.

Her 447 days would come to $2.4 million—our share, just short of three thousand dollars, for the ambulance that took her from General to the Clinic. (We hadn't chosen the company, didn't know we had a choice. We did, and her plan didn't cover the one that took her.) It wasn't simply her being a municipal employee but a municipal employee in Akron, where, thanks to rubber, unionization had entrenched itself early on in the public sector as well. As a result, her coverage was first-rate: a two-million-dollar cap plus an additional million that came with disability.

However, as Dad had deduced from going over the thirty-plus-page invoices arriving at the house at least once a week, what a hospital charges for a service isn't what the insurance company ends up paying. There's negotiating that takes place for everything, and what one provider is willing to pony up might be more or less than another. (One of her bronchs, for instance. The Clinic charged $2,525. The insurance company paid $461.31.) I guessed Mom's was stingier than most and that the case manager was protecting the bottom line, trying to run us out the same as a waiter would a party not drinking and ordering the cheapest entrées on the menu.

Before the LTAC talk got too serious, though, the shifting of the trach was discovered, weaning got back on track, and the case manager disappeared. For another month or so, anyway.

III.

Oxygen saturation level, or sats (the measure of oxygen-carrying red blood cell), and heart rate were read by the pulsox worn on her right index finger; sometimes the plastic clip-on kind, other times the adhesive version, which would get grimy and start to smell after a week or so but would stay on for three weeks or longer. It was connected by a wire to a waist-high monitor on wheels next to the vent. Sometimes the wire would get snagged on the bottom guardrail we always kept lowered and she wouldn't be able to move her arm.

Breaths per minute and $ETCO_2$ (end tidals) were read by a capnometer, a black cube attached to the vent hose and connected by a wire to a small monitor atop the vent. Because of the cube's heft, it would be left off when she was on the trach collar, a spot check done once an hour instead.

Displayed in waveform on the vent's touch screen were the ones I couldn't begin to make sense of then and certainly can't now—tidal volume, FiO_2, PEEP.

The numbers.

Almost always were they trusted over the patient's word. And understandably. No say in what meds they're getting or when they're getting them, what procedure they're undergoing or when they'll be taken for it. Even something as basic as what time they wake up: Every morning at five Mom was roused to have labs drawn, and, if she was lucky enough to fall back asleep, she'd be disturbed again around six thirty by the doctors on rounds. Ambien at midnight, labs at five almost every night for more than nine months. Midnight because if she took it any earlier she'd just be woken then anyway when the aides pricked her finger for blood sugar and the nurses stuck her belly with insulin—the skin like a moonscape, blackish blue and pockmarked. Besides TV, weaning is pretty much the only opportunity for patients to impose their will. Thus their demands to be put back on full support when sats are 99 or even 100 percent. It's a control thing.

Or anxiety. Over time the mind becomes as reliant on the vent as the lungs. And as with any such security blanket, being deprived of it is horrifying. The only way patients will get over this fear and anxiety, the thinking held, is if they recognize it for what it is. And the only way they'll do *this* is by going longer than they think they can—even if only a few minutes—and seeing that everything's okay, that they're still there, that the bottom didn't drop out after all. You push them through it.

And if that doesn't work—as I'd always argue, what does it matter if the heart rate's in the 130s due to mere anxiety or real fatigue, it's still in the 130s, isn't it?—resort to more clandestine measures. Decrease support without telling them or when they're asleep. When they're asleep or gone from the room for a procedure, take the clock from the wall and set it back five minutes. Measures I completely endorsed and even served as accomplice to: When Mom got wise and asked if they'd changed her vent settings, I denied it, and when the truth came out, I played dumb. So many times. So many times my patience would run low and I'd lean in and look her in the eye and say sternly, "You're fine. Okay? *You're fine.* Your numbers are perfect. It's just anxiety. You gotta get over this shit, Mom. You got enough problems without causing any more." See her trying to push the call button and not having the strength or dexterity but refusing to do it for her, knowing she was just wanting respiratory, who'd just been in two seconds before and was just going to say the same thing.

So how terrible did I feel when the day before Valentine's and the Ilgauskases' miscarriage, they did a bronch—her fifth so far—and found the trach to have been somehow jostled out of place, jamming into the esophageal wall, more than half the aperture closed off? While the numbers somehow hadn't technically been incorrect, less than half the amount of air she was supposed to be getting at any one time was making it through. For how long, who knows.

My self-disgust was compounded a couple days later. It was snowing heavily, and though I tried almost a dozen times to get up the brick hill, I finally gave up and called reSCU, told her nurse to let her know I wouldn't be coming. The first night I'd miss since she'd arrived at the Clinic.

In addition to cutting back on the hospital visits, Dad's doctor had recommended more exercise. So on top of his usual pickup games two or three afternoons a week with high school kids at a local gym, he began playing tennis every Thursday night at the Valley's indoor courts—this enormous, lit-up white bubble in the middle of the woods that always creeped me out as kid, made me think of aliens and covert governmental experiments crossbreeding animals. This was a Thursday. Dad met me at the bridge so I could take his car and get food for dinner. I just had to pick him up after tennis.

As I waited in the parking lot for him to come out, I started crying. Then I started beating on the steering wheel, slamming it with the heel of my hands, throttling and shaking it so hard I'm surprised

I didn't yank it straight off. By the time Dad got in the car I'd worn myself out, but he could tell something was up and when he asked I started crying again.

"She's up there all alone," I said. "She's up there and I'm stuck here."

"She understands," he said. "It's okay. It's just one night. You'll see her tomorrow."

"But what if I don't? What if something happens tonight?"

"What? You think it wouldn't if you were there?"

"No, but at least I'd be there. At least she wouldn't have to face whatever it is all by herself."

"It's out of your control, Sean. None of us control any of this shit. You're doing the best you can but you can only do so much."

I wouldn't miss another night the rest of her time at the Clinic. And that snowfall was nothing compared to how northeastern Ohio would get slammed over the next couple months, well into April, when the Indians had all four games of their opening home stand snowed out and, with conditions still not improving, were forced to move their next scheduled home series to Milwaukee. There were a few nights I didn't even try driving home—just curled up in the high-backed chair, or, if Mom was in an ICU, stretched out on its waiting area's floor, using my coat for a pillow—and many more when about halfway there I'd realize it would've been wiser to have done the same. You couldn't tell where the road was, just had to follow the taillights of the car in front of you the same as they were doing with the car in front of them and hope whoever was up there leading the pack didn't go into a ditch. You had to stay right up on each other, too—visibility less than five feet, the stuff coming down so thick and fast it was like the *Millennium Falcon* going into hyperspace, complete and total whiteouts. Talk about throttling the steering wheel—it'd take a while after I got home for my fingers to uncramp and release their claw shape.

But I always got home. It'd take me two hours sometimes, but I'd always make it. That's what leaves me wondering about that cosmic dispensation, if there weren't something keeping me safe after all. Seventy miles a day for more than a year, no driving experience in the previous five besides the catering van a few times a month, and not a single accident, not one blown tire or speeding ticket. (Just in case, I kept in my wallet a Patrolmen's Benevolent Association card Sully had given me: "Don't make a big show of it. Just make sure it's somewhere they can see it when you pull out your license.")

I didn't exercise or belong to a gym in New York but at least had all that walking and those subway stairs. That and work—lifting coolers full of food and dry lugs of chef's equipment, buckets of ice and rented convection ovens and cases of wine. Now I'd just go from sitting in the car to sitting in the room back to sitting in the car. Once I'd found the Clinic's stairs, I started taking those instead of the elevator. I don't think I was supposed to. I'm pretty sure the stairwell was just for doctors: That's all I ever saw using it. Some of the floors had combination locks, and it came out well into the F Building in a narrow hallway lined with offices. But even more bizarre than the presence of McDonald's, there was no staircase for the public. I'd also take the stairs in P1. Combined, though, those twenty or so flights a day were hardly enough to counteract all the junk I was eating.

While she was in G-53 and my hours were still somewhat regular, my diet wasn't so bad—the salad bar for lunch and for dinner usually some soup and a Caesar salad. When she got to reSCU and I started my four thirty to twelve thirty schedule, however, the cafeteria buffets would be closed for the dinner changeover by the time I got there, so for lunch I'd either get tacos from La Salsa or on my way up stop and grab a sandwich at a bagel place in the Valley— even more amazing I never got in an accident, since sometimes I was too hungry to wait to get to the room and ate while steering with my knees. I still hadn't adjusted to grocery shopping a week in advance or to the absence of around-the-clock bodegas with fresh produce and organic everything, and by the time I'd make it back to Akron the only place still open would be Walgreen's. So dinner, then— until late in the spring, when I discovered Fairlawn's twenty-four-hour Giant Eagle—would be either a Stouffer's meat lasagna or a Weight Watchers pepperoni pizza. Once in a while I'd stop down at Luigi's for the real thing—they were open till two during the week. On weekends Swenson's was open till one, and either Friday or Saturday I'd get burgers and fries. The only healthy meals I ever had were the one or two weekends a month Elaine was in and cooked.

All the kisses I gave Mom when she had thrush. All the times she'd get C. diff and, not wanting to make her feel insecure, I'd refuse to wear the plastic gown and mask. (Even Claire, who ordinarily would balk at obscuring her pearls and mussing her hair with so tacky a getup, put them on.) Yet I never got sick. It's crazy, especially considering how worn down my immune system must've been under all that stress and with so little rest.

Mostly what you had was on the agitated side of half-sleep, you thought you were sleeping but you were really just waiting.

Dispatches again, and exactly how it was with me. By the time I ate, called Elaine, and read, it'd be close to four, then up again by ten thirty, eleven. Never sleeping deeply enough to dream. Subconsciously waiting for that phone to ring, keeping both the landline and my cell on the bedside table. Still, that was better than the week of nonstop throwing up when I stayed in the room every night and hardly closed my eyes at all.

Seriously, how awful must it have been to be hospitalized before TV? We got a taste of it when one afternoon early on in the X-Box the power went out. Generators kept the equipment running but the TV wouldn't turn on. Two or three hours it lasted, me just standing there rubbing Mom's head and her wide awake with nothing for distraction.

I can't even imagine how much more miserable those five nights to end February and begin March would've been without Nick at Nite. The bed fully upright. Flipping over her forehead washcloth after ten minutes and refreshing it every twenty. Her chin resting on the paper bucket, it trembling in her hands. The gagging and heaving coming every ten, fifteen minutes. The tube feed long shut off, nothing left but viscous green stomach acid that I'd wipe from her lips and chin with tissues. With another balled-up wad, wiping away her tears. And the whole time her eyes fixed on the one-hour, two-hour, sometimes all-night blocks of *The Fresh Prince of Bel-Air* and *The Cosby Show, Home Improvement* and *Roseanne.* The volume on the handset turned up as loud as it'd go.

This was just after they'd fixed the trach and she'd got up to five and a half hours off the vent. All sorts of tests and scans, checking

her liver, her gall bladder, everything negative. Claire coming up a
little earlier than usual, around nine. Me going home for a few
hours' sleep then returning by seven. The bleach-blond nurse my
age who a month or so later would take a job in South Carolina
where her army boyfriend was stationed, with us all week except
one night she was off, her telling Mom the next, "I called up last
night to check on you. Yeah, I couldn't sleep and was laying in bed
flipping through the channels and saw *The Fresh Prince* on and
thought, Let me see how Ms. Manning's doing." Giving her morphine for the stabbing pain in her side.

Then all of a sudden it stops, she's fine, fantastic. Monday,
March 5: *Great Day! When I arrived this morning physical
therapy was exercising her legs. He asked her if she would
like to sit up on the side of the bed. She said yes. After
sitting for a while he asked if she would like to stand. She
said yes. After standing for a short time she took her first
steps!*

That was one thing the LTACs had over reSCU. Like the rest of
reSCU's staff, the physical therapists covering the unit were non-
pareil, especially the one who worked with her the most, Matt—
shaved head, early forties, he and his wife in the process of adopting
a baby from China. He was always real patient, let Mom go at her
own pace so long as she didn't cut corners, made sure she always
brought her legs and arms all the way up or out and did all the reps
in a set. That was about all he or any of the other physical therapists
could do, stretch her and do basic strengthening exercises with her
in bed—because she was on the vent and couldn't go anywhere. But
even if she wasn't, there wasn't anywhere to go anyway, no special
PT rooms like in the LTACs, rooms filled with elastic bands and

big rubber balls and two-pound dumbbells and, at Grace, this big, medieval rack-looking metal contraption patients long bedridden would be strapped into in order to regain the balance and core strength needed to resume walking.

The third week of March, with her up to twelve hours on the trach collar and everything looking fairly stable, one of the staff doctors again raised the idea of transfer. We were more receptive than before—especially as it was coming from a doctor rather than an administrator—and I went ahead and checked out a couple more LTACs. Originally, the case manager had mentioned only General's and Summa's, thinking we'd want to be closer to home. I told her we didn't care where it was, so long as it was the best one—what was the best one? She couldn't say, some sort of regulation preventing her. All she could do was give me an expanded list to include places in and around Cleveland.

Though also operated by the Grace corporation, the LTAC in Lakewood Hospital—another Clinic affiliate—didn't seem any better than those in Akron. Grace Fairview, though, I instantly felt good about. Occupying the hospital's sixth and topmost floor, the carpeted unit was far quieter and less chaotic than reSCU, the spacious private rooms with beautiful cherrywood floors and picture windows looking out, most of them, onto the maples and oaks and beeches and cottonwoods of Cleveland Metroparks' neighboring Rocky River Reservation. The all-important nurse-to-patient ratio was something like one-to-four—not quite reSCU's one-to-two, but no worse than that of the other LTACs. Plus there was the location. Situated among the suburbs of Lakewood, just west of Cleveland, it was all of ten miles from the Main Campus—a quick ambulance ride should something else happen to her heart. And while Dr. Graham would no longer be managing the cancer treatment—unless she got well enough to see him on an outpatient basis—at least with another Clinic-affiliated oncologist, as opposed to one from General or Summa, there'd be some continuity of care.

Mom was pleased by my report. However, we both agreed not to initiate anything, to wait till the case manager or doctors really started bearing down on us. The more weaning she could get done in reSCU, the quicker she could dive into physical therapy at Grace, the more productive her time there would be.

That weekend Claire brought up her hairdresser to give Mom a trim and a real shampoo. Since that shower back in October, her hair was washed using a no-rinse cap a couple times a week. Every morning her body was washed—wiped down, really—by the aides with a washcloth and a basin of soapy water. It didn't take long. She was down to around 120 pounds, about 30 less than she usually weighed, though still 10 or so more than where she'd end up. However blighted the rest of her looked, though, her face remained as youthful as it'd always been. "Not a wrinkle," Dad marveled more than one Sunday night before leaving. "Looks the same as when she was twenty."

IV.

It was around then that Walsh's quarterly magazine arrived at the house. Usually I'd read the alumni notes then throw it away. This time I also scanned the In Memoriam section. I was just curious if anybody from my year or near it had recently lost a parent, and so was stunned to find Charles's name.

He'd been a grade ahead. I wasn't good friends with him, but I'd been to his house a few times to hang out and shoot pool. It was an enormous house even by Walsh standards—private drive, enough acreage for an ATV. Yet Charles was so down-to-earth, you'd never have guessed. I figured his name listed in the quarterly was some mistake, some proofreading gaffe, supposed to have been his grandfather or something. If it'd been Charles, I'd have heard about it.

Just to be sure, I called Ben.

"Hey, man, this is kind of a . . . a . . . Did Charles *die*?"

"Fuck. I didn't tell you."

"No. Jesus. When was this?"

"Last summer."

"What happened?"

"He had some sort of stomach cancer. It happened pretty fast."

Up through high school, I never had a friend or classmate die or get some life-threatening illness. None of their brothers or sisters or parents died or got sick. Actually, I doubt any of my friends knew Mom had had cancer, so maybe I was similarly in the dark about their folks. Regardless, whether real or imagined, growing up I was unacquainted with tragedy.

I don't mean loss. That I knew decent enough. Grandma Hesidence, Grandma Manning, Patchie—Dad weeping there in the backyard as he placed her chew toy and a Polaroid of the four of us on top of the garbage bag he'd brought her back from the vet's in and said a few words about what a wonderful friend she'd been before taking up the shovel and filling in the hole. But those could be foreseen. Even Aunt Julia's heart attack. Awful, fucking awful. Family would never be the same. Yet there was the family history—Grandpa's own heart attack. No, I mean never-saw-it-coming tragedy—I wouldn't become familiar with that till the summer after freshman year of college, till Paige.

I can still remember the day we went out in sixth grade. Literally, a day—I asked her that morning, we talked on the phone that night for about twenty minutes, and by the next day's lunch she'd dumped me. I was too much of a prude. Paige thought Doo-Wops and Continentals were for pussies, was just how she'd have put it, had a filthier mouth than any of us guys and was a better belcher, too. I still have a group picture from the last day of eighth grade. The twenty or so of us who hung out—went to the movies every Friday night, to the big cineplex out past the mall, and afterward to the Taco Bell or McDonald's across Market till Mom or one of the other parents picked us up—all smiling and jumping on one another's shoulders to be seen. Paige scowling, long, dirty-blond hair blowing across her face, giving the finger. She was one of those rapping the loudest along to "Baby Got Back" on the bus ride to D.C. I got her the cassette of Nirvana's *Nevermind* for her seventh-grade birthday party. (Mom fought me on that one—did *not* approve of the cover. But as our deal was "no parental-advisory stickers" and not "no naked babies swimming after dollar bills," she ultimately relented.)

Paige was one of only a couple Litchfield girls who went to Walsh. We'd drift apart, too, but if we had lunch the same period we would still sit at the same table, and she didn't hesitate to give me a hard time about my thrift-store duds. There was always that bond from having known each other so long, always would be.

It was one of the Firestone High girls who called and told me. Actually, she was calling for Mom. Hers was out of town, and a few other girls from the old group had spent the night, and they were all having a hard time keeping it together. They'd always adored Mom—more than any of the other parents felt close to and comfortable with her. When she got home, she gave me a hug and said if I felt like talking she was there but then let me be, didn't press it. Later that day the flowers first appeared on Merriman Road, nailed to the tree. I'd pass it every day on my way to the Clinic. Somebody still put flowers there. Every few months a new bouquet would be nailed up.

V.

Tuesday, March 27. Mom's sixth-month anniversary in the Clinic. That morning she reached another milestone: twenty-four hours on the trach collar. (I was there for it, staying in the room as I always did on her first attempt at weaning overnight.) In reSCU, you weren't considered officially weaned until seventy-two hours, and thus far the protocol had been kept extremely conservative, only pushing her an extra hour or two each night. Once past that twenty-four mark, however, she was presumed to be over the hump and able to just keep going. So she was left on the collar, and at 1:30 ––– *hit the fan. Started non-stop coughing+throwing up. Suctioning often but continued all afternoon. Finally, Dr. came in+ordered her back on the vent; starting antibiotics (fever); stopping tube feeding; ordering CT of the chest ...possible pneumonia.*

The next day her blood pressure once again dropped and she was transferred to an ICU on the sixth floor of the H Building for a night and then to one on the second floor of the G Building for a few more. By early the following week she was back in reSCU. Unfortunately, either that week or the next happened to be Dr. Daniels's turn in the rotation.

My contempt for him made that which Walsh and St. V had for each other seem like veneration. He was the oldest of reSCU's half dozen staff doctors, in his late sixties. His face had this puckered, disagreeable look as if he'd just taken a bite of something tart. His posture was so rigid he seemed to be bending backward. He always wore a different argyle sweater vest, and, given my reaction to Dr. Graham's glasses, you can guess how well that went over. Yet Dr. Graham was simply being fashionable; with Dr. Daniels it seemed more a craving for notoriety, an attempt to set himself apart even beyond the white coat and black lettering. His *real* hallmark was the edginess that never failed to envelop the floor upon his appearance, the sudden coolness of the staff and desistance of banter both among themselves and with us. So far we'd experienced about half a dozen of these on-pins-and-needles weeks, and I'd often seen him in the waiting-area chairs holding court with two or three fawning acolyte residents.

"Yet this is the first time I've seen you in her room," I said that afternoon he stopped by. "I know I get here late and you round in the morning, but still. You can see how I might have a hard time putting a whole lot of faith in what you're saying."

What he was saying was that it was time—time for her to move. I stated my case—how the risk of infection didn't seem any less, how with only thirty days she was a shoo-in for skilled nursing, how no LTAC would be able to do a better job getting her off the vent than reSCU.

"Unless you just think she won't be able to," I said.

I can't remember when I put it together, if just then or days, maybe weeks, earlier. Granted, I wasn't 100 percent sure. Nor am I now—the journal doesn't mention who was the doctor on rotation that week the case manager first started pushing. But it seemed to make sense—that it'd been him, and that the real reason wasn't the money after all but Dr. Daniels's overwhelming lack of confidence in Mom. Except rather than say so himself he'd left it to the case manager, and she'd chosen to be more politic.

Not this time. This time I was going to make him do it. And in front of Mom—why I declined his invitation to speak in the hall. I wanted her to hear it, knew how much it'd piss her off, thought it might be just the spark she needed to get back on track.

"Well," he said, "given her history, I think we need to consider that a good possibility."

"Right, well, okay, but if it's only a possibility, then you're saying there's also the possibility she still might be able to. Right?"

"At this point, I think it's unlikely."

Even surmising he thought so, wanting him to say it, putting as little stock in his opinion as I did, it still hurt to hear. But it had the desired effect. Mom's eyes burned with indignation. She'd do it. I knew she would. She just needed time.

"Okay," I said. "All right. But before she goes, GI mentioned a while back putting in a G-tube. A J-tube, too. Could we maybe look into doing that first?"

CHAPTER NINE

I.

The pulsox's alarm tripped when sats fell below 92 percent—I freaked at anything less than 96—and heart rate exceeded 135 beats per minute, or when, because of Mom's poor circulation, made even worse by how cold she liked the room kept, the infrared failed to pick up a signal. I forget what levels triggered the capnometer's alarm. The vent's alarm sounded whenever she went into one of her minute-long, face-purpling coughing fits—made me grit my teeth and white-knuckle the chair's armrests every time—or when condensation forced the hose nozzle off the trach. I'd hear the whoosh of air even before the alarm could start and scramble to fit it back on.

The first two alarms I could silence myself by pushing a button. For the vent's, if it didn't stop on its own, we'd have to wait for the RT, sometimes a few minutes if they were busy. In order to be heard out in the hall, it was piercing. I'd forgotten what it sounded like until recently when I listened to the tape of the conversation with Drs. Graham and Waters. The couple times it went off in the background were even harder to bear than what they were saying.

In his early forties, short, with thinning, close-cropped hair, glasses, and a goatee, Dr. Waters was the staff doctor I was most impressed with, calling as he did to notify me of the PET-scan results—the infiltrated lymph node as well as the resurgent mass in the lung. However, it could've been worse. The biopsy on the mass in her esophagus was negative—again, likely just scar tissue from intubation or extubation.

He'd spoken with Dr. Graham. Since the cancer remained localized, further radiation was an option. But Dr. Waters wanted everybody to understand exactly what she'd be in for. He asked us to meet in her room to discuss—himself, Dr. Graham, Claire, and me. Since Roger was out of town, Claire, conscientious as ever, suggested I pick up one of those little recorders, the same sort Mom had used for her U of A lectures. That way if he had any questions, nothing would be lost in translation.

There was no need; Roger never listened to it. And just as well, since I failed to flip over the tape. I would have had to let go of her hand, and hell if I was going to do that. Not that what was said in those fifteen, twenty minutes after the tape ran out was anything that hadn't already been covered in the first thirty. In fact, much of *that* was just the doctors going over the same ground, rephrasing the same answers to my same rephrased questions that I already knew the answers to and was just asking to keep them talking, keep them in the room, knowing she'd be less frightened with them nearby.

She'd started sobbing as soon as she learned the PET results.

Me: *It's okay, all right? Let him finish, all right? They're here to figure everything out, okay?*

The doctors, too, did their best to reassure her.

Dr. Waters: *I'm not . . . I'm not trying to get you down here. I don't see anything that tells me that we're at that point where we have to stop, the point of medical futility where nothing I do is gonna make a difference—I don't see any of that.*

Dr. Graham: *You say are you terminal* [the only question she'd ask]. *What terminal to me means. . . . When I talk to someone about that, that means I know that they've gotta understand that their disease is really serious, I'll help them as much as I can, and I'll do everything I can, but I talk about it so that they have . . . they don't get frightened and they think, What's gonna happen in the next couple days or the next couple weeks? This isn't you. We're not talking about tomorrow or a week from now, that you're terminal, and that's the way I hear that word. . . . You're at no risk from the cancer right now. You're at no risk.*

Dr. Waters: *If you weren't a fighter, you wouldn't be here right now. I'm sure of that. We're gonna help you along as much as we can. I don't want you to think that I'm having this talk because I think it's time to pull the plug.*

Yet they didn't sugarcoat it. They needed her to know precisely where things stood, what a clusterfuck it was—heart, cancer, stomach, vent—and what a near insurmountable challenge it'd be going forward.

The hope had been to eradicate the tumor with those first two radiation sessions. With the cancer spreading, the likelihood of further radiation doing the trick was far less: at most 5 percent, the doctors estimated. Rather, its purpose would be to buy her time—six months, more or less—to get off the vent and get stronger and healthy enough for chemo. That was her only shot. If she wanted to take it.

It was then that hospice was first mentioned.

> Dr. Waters: *It's not just for someone who's immediately going to die. There's the entire spectrum, from backing off just a little bit, not having anything additional, to complete and total comfort care where we're talking about the morphine drip and stopping the ventilator. There's a wide range of where that can be. . . . There are a lot of different versions. There's in a hospital hospice, there's in a hospice hospice, and an at-home hospice. Now, on a ventilator, at-home hospice becomes much more difficult. But . . . there's no one set way that hospice is or has to be.*

After the doctors left, Claire moved from the foot of the bed where she'd been stroking Mom's legs to the near side where the doctors had stood, took her hand, and rubbed her forehead and said a prayer. Then she kissed her and left us to be alone. I talked for a while, don't remember about what, just filling the silence. Mom wasn't listening, just staring off, trapped in her head.

"Anxiety," she finally mouthed.

Dr. Waters had agreed to let her have her Klonopin a couple hours early. I called the nurse and asked for it.

"You don't have to decide tonight," I told her while we waited. "Or even tomorrow. You've got some time."

By the next morning she'd made up her mind.

Friday, June 8: *She is sleeping when I arrived. Woke up when nurse comes in to get blood pressure. I have a talk with her. Basically I question her about her choice of options knowing she has definitely suffered for 8 months. She emphatically tells me, "I choose life!" Wants to continue to fight! Started weaning—was off for one hour.*

II.

The Clinic's let's-do-everything-we-can-to-make-the-place-not-feel-like-a-hospital policy—and it *was* a policy ". . . medical equipment is hidden as often as possible," wrote their "Chief Experience Officer" in a June 2008 blog post introducing the new heart center—wouldn't bother me so much if I thought it was meant to put the patients and their loved ones at ease rather than the trustees or prospective benefactors or summit attendees or media corps at their press conferences (such as the one I caught on the news the other night unveiling the recipient of the first-ever face transplant—which, I won't deny, is fucking incredible). And I wouldn't think this if such a stink hadn't been made about the detour I'd proposed for the trip to her first radiation session, on July 2.

Since the T Building was right by the main entrance, I thought we might go outside and then come back in—*straight* back in, without stopping—through an exterior side entrance to the radiation and oncology department. All of thirty seconds and fifty feet of sidewalk, but what a lift to her spirits—feeling the sun on her face and arms, remembering what she was working so hard for. The staff doctor thought it was a terrific idea, and Mom had gotten all excited in the couple days prior. I'd even brought in her sunglasses so she wouldn't have to squint. Cloudless, a slight breeze—you couldn't have asked for better weather to do it.

When I told transport the plan, however, they were wary, said they'd have to call their boss, who told them no.

"They don't let beds or ventilator patients through the main entrance," the guy who'd called explained. "You have to be in a wheel-chair."

"Bullshit," I said. "What's your boss's extension?"

When I got him on the phone, he said the same thing.

"Look," I said, "this woman hasn't been out of the hospital in nine months. Do you hear me? *Nine months.* Not once outside, not for a single second. I know you're just following orders, so tell me who I have to talk to to make it happen. Who's your boss? What's his number?"

The boss ultimately okayed it, turned out to be real decent, insisted on coming along should any higher-up give us grief. And to make sure they didn't have the opportunity, he took us—Mom, me, the two transport guys, and the RT pushing the portable vent—on a circuitous route even more all-access than had been our entrance to the Clinic that very first night. The double-wide G Building patient elevators down to some dungeon of a sub-basement. Up and down steep ramps. Through dingy passages at times so low-ceilinged we practically had to duck and so narrow the RT had to swing the vent behind Mom's head and go through single file. The gurney angled into a tiny service elevator with room for only the boss and RT, me and the transport guys left to take the stairs.

Finally, somehow, we emerged amid those portraits of former presidents. To the quizzical looks of the greeters, unused to the sight of a patient supine, we passed through the main entrance and, after I quickly slipped the sunglasses on Mom, outside. Never have I seen such a look of contentment, her smile even more radiant than the day.

"Thank you," she mouthed as we waited for the nurses to take her into the radiation room, then again after we'd returned to reSCU and she was back in bed, and once more before I left that night.

I saw the radiation room once: the same honey-colored wood on the walls as on the floor, nothing except the table and machine overhead, softly lit, soothing New Age music piped in. She'd undergo ten sessions, although she'd make eleven trips. Once a delay made her wait so long that the back pain caused by the gurney forced her to return to reSCU. It had to be a gurney; the radiation and oncology elevator was too narrow to fit the inflatable mattress. I'd put a pillow under her knees but that only helped a little. Another time when there was a longer than usual delay the RT called up to have her nurse bring more morphine. (She was always given some before going down.) The actual session only took twenty, twenty-five minutes, but between waiting to go in and afterward for transport to show—as in G-53, the radiation nurses would put in the request for pickup the moment she arrived—it usually took about an hour, hour and a half. She'd be on full support throughout, but as soon as she got back to reSCU and settled into bed it was right back to weaning.

She didn't finish until July 20. By the thirty-first, she was up to two days on the trach collar. So as to avoid another crash, the staff doctor on rotation that week decided to let her rest on the vent overnight and back off about an hour each night over the next week or so.

The strategy paid off. Despite muscle pain in her chest that led to an inconclusive X-ray (she averaged about three per week), the discovery of another pneumonia that had the RTs rolling her on her side and using a vibrating massager on her back to break it up, and, as always, the constant problems with her Corpak and IVs, she got up to five days off the vent and on August 17 was moved out of reSCU.

Originally, the plan was to move her to a step-down floor, but I raised hell. She still needed frequent suctioning, some days as often as every ten, fifteen minutes. No way could a step-down floor with its one-to-four or -five nurse-to-patient ratio afford her that much attention. So—and I have to give him this much at least—Dr. Daniels agreed to let her stay in one of the couple single-occupancy rooms reserved for infectious-disease patients just a couple doors down the hall and served by the reSCU staff until such a patient was admitted or Mom's transfer to an LTAC could be arranged. He was pushing for the move harder than ever, saying we should anticipate it happening the following week, but we knew by then not to get too worked up, that once he rotated off, the talk would die down. And anyway no LTAC would take her with pneumonia, and that'd be more like two weeks before fully clearing up.

In the meantime, her trach was replaced with a smaller one able to be capped with a Passy-Muir valve. This allowed her to talk while still breathing through the trach. Even so, it was a strain; rarely was she able to make it all the way through the deck of flash cards Claire ran with her each day. And her voice was faint and throaty. But it was her voice all right, for the first time since November, and damn, was it wonderful to hear—hear, for instance, her excitement over the pictures Dad showed her of the backyard.

Thinking it'd give her some motivation or at least provide a distraction, Dad—with his own money—had replaced the rotting railroad-tie staircase leading from the basketball court to the small plateau of lawn off the patio and deck. That patch of grass as well as the larger back slope that always funneled airballs down into the neighbors' yard (except when nestling in the lip where Patchie was buried) had been in bad shape the last few years, so in addition Dad had all that taken up and new topsoil, seed, and straw laid. He turned the sprinkler on every afternoon, and when the grass came up he mowed it.

If it sometimes seemed Dad had never left, that was another reason—seeing him back out there in the yard. Also, the nurses and doctors referring to him as Mom's husband. At first he would correct them. But from then on they'd sort of look at him strange, unable to square how he could always be there and the two of them be so loving toward each other, unsure if they should talk to him or not, how much information they should or were allowed to share. It made him furious. "Husband, ex-husband," he said once. "What the hell does it matter? That supposed to mean we don't love each other?" So after a while he quit saying anything.

The few times I've talked to him about it recently, about how uncommon their relationship was, he's said it was only thanks to me, that otherwise they probably would've lost touch after the divorce. I don't buy it. Once I was out of college and the last tuition payment had been made, the two of them no longer had any official business and could've easily drifted apart. They didn't, were as close as ever. She was the first person he told about buying his house, the first to see it. Around the time he was finishing the remodel, she found a sleeper sofa, chair, and ottoman set for the rec room at a local furniture store. "They're having a big sale," she told him. "You should go check it out, see if there's anything you like. We can save on delivery—just do it ourselves." He also found a sleeper sofa, and that's just what they did—rented a U-Haul one Saturday and moved it all in. Her stuff went fine, but when they were bringing in his sofa, just as they got inside, his back gave out and he dropped it, putting a huge gash in the brand-new hardwood. Fortunately, he now had something on which to recuperate. But what it cost to repair the floor wound up being twice what they'd have paid for delivery.

No, the only way things might've ever changed between them is if either had remarried. And what would this whole experience have been like then? How would that have affected Dad's level of involvement? As a matter of fact, he was in a relationship, a serious one, going on five or six years. It's not my place to discuss it, that's something I'm definitely not comfortable doing. And even if I were, I don't know nearly enough to—only met her a couple times. But to make no mention of it at all would be an even more flagrant abstention than to have done so with Grandpa Manning's drinking—of how hard it was on him caring so deeply for Mom and wanting to be there for her and me but the emotional strain it put him under, how that contributed to his and his girlfriend's breakup. Just saying that little I feel I've overstepped my bounds, and I apologize, Dad, to you and her both. I just think it's important to acknowledge how messy this shit gets, the collateral damage or whatever. But then, I don't need your relationship to make that point. I've got my own.

III.

Those fourteen months or so I'd thought about myself as little as possible so that I could focus all my energy on Mom. I lived solely to help her. The same went for Elaine—her existence came to revolve around supporting me. Only she had it far worse. At least Mom was there, I could see what a help I was being, could kiss and hug her and hold her hand, got some return comfort from that. Plus I had all the others for support. Like a lot of couples in their first year of living together, Elaine and I had stopped going out as much with friends, sort of sequestered ourselves. And then one day I'm gone, no idea when I might be back, leaving her without anyone to lean on. Getting to spend maybe six days out of the month with me and most of those nights at the hospital. The rest of the time on the phone, not knowing if what she was saying was doing any good and figuring probably not by the way I was acting. It was the same as why I didn't journal—at the end of the night the last thing I wanted to do was replay what had happened. And since that's all my life was, I didn't have much to say, made her do all the talking.

That didn't change when I came back to New York. I didn't return to catering, didn't reach out to my magazine contacts or begin on my Young Man from the Provinces novel. I figured that'd just add to my frustration over my feeling that nothing had changed, that the last year and a half had had no effect on the world, that I was stuck in a time warp even more eerie than that *Happy Days* episode in which I'd grown up. This was a mistake, I realize now. If not catering or writing, I should've gotten some other job, something to get me out of the house and interacting with people. Instead I just lived off what I didn't invest of Mom's life-insurance payout and the balance of her pension and sat on the couch in my underwear and read—the Roth and Didion and Herr, and went on this whole Norman Mailer kick after he died, including *Studs Lonigan* after learning in an obituary it'd been one of his biggest influences.

So that when Elaine got home from work, other than how we took our eye off the ball at Khe Sanh or what a tease that Lucy Scanlon was, I wouldn't have much to contribute in the way of conversation.

And whereas after her long day she understandably just wanted to crash and watch *Gossip Girl* or *30 Rock*, I'd be going stir-crazy, desperate to get out of the apartment, had watched enough TV in the hospital to last three lifetimes. I'd take half-hour walks up to Ditmars Boulevard or down Thirtieth Avenue with its open-air Greek cafés and patrons sitting outside sipping iced coffees even in mid-December, but that did more harm than good, just gave me more time by myself, more of a chance to contemplate who I was, what I wanted, if it was indeed okay to want, if I shouldn't just be grateful for my health and my wonderful girlfriend, friends, and family. Why couldn't I be grateful for everything I still had rather than bitter over what I'd lost?

Bitter and angry. I'd begun to snap at Elaine for the littlest things, can't even remember what, that's how stupid they were. A lot of times it'd be nothing she did or anything that triggered it; I'd just all of a sudden find myself in a rage, storm into the bedroom, slam the door, go a round or two with the mattress and scream into a pillow. After a while I joined a gym, hoping that might be the answer—for my sleeplessness, too. I hadn't been able to break the hospital schedule. Plus I couldn't look at a bed anymore without seeing a shackle: Lying in one made me feel trapped and anxious. I'd read some more till three or four, then finally turn in. Even then I couldn't really fall asleep until Elaine was up and I heard the shower running—still in that by-shifts mentality. Working out helped, but only a little.

She was still as understanding and supportive as ever, didn't take it too personally when I flew off the handle, knew what it was about and just let me vent. But eventually—right around the year anniversary, in fact, though how much that had to do with it I'm not sure—I realized, we both did, how unhealthy this was for her . . . for me, as taking it out on her just made me feel guilty and even worse than I did to begin with, but especially for her. She needed to wrestle with all those same questions I was wrestling with, only I wasn't letting her, was keeping her locked in that same role she'd occupied all those months. So we agreed to take some time apart, and here I am sitting at the kitchen table of a studio apartment no bigger than one of Mom's reSCU rooms.

Elaine was wonderful with Mom, would sit there giving her ten-, fifteen-minute hand massages that put her to sleep. If the nurses were slow to respond to the call light when Mom started throwing up, Elaine would go looking for them while I stayed and held the bucket and wiped her chin. When we'd leave for the night, she'd kiss Mom and squeeze her hand and tell her she loved her and would see her in a couple weeks. Mom was just the same with Grandma Manning those last few years of her life when she was in a nursing home with Alzheimer's. Grandma would start stuttering incoherently and banging her hand on the arm of her wheelchair and Mom would clap in time and turn the gibberish into a song and Grandma would laugh. It was all the more touching given—according to Mom, anyway—that Grandma never liked her, thought Dad could've done better. Mom felt completely the opposite about Elaine. "You're a fool if you let her go," she mouthed to me one afternoon in reSCU after I'd shared with her how shut-down I was being on the phone and how I sometimes wondered if Elaine wouldn't be better off without me, without this mess in her life. "A damn fool."

Whenever Mom was feeling halfway decent, she insisted that Elaine and I leave early, around eight or nine, and go out to dinner. We did a couple times, once to this great Mexican place in Cleveland Heights Elaine had wanted to try. And one afternoon before going up we caught a matinee of the splatterfest *Grindhouse*—closer to a romantic comedy compared with all the carnage I'd seen. But that was pretty much it, the extent of my socializing. After Sully was turned away by Mom, I didn't see him again until hospice. After spending that night at Ben's, didn't see him until calling hours. I did talk to them on the phone, as well as to some of the catering guys and other friends from New York—usually after one in the morning or so, when I was at the Giant Eagle.

My car would be one of only five or six in the lot, the others belonging to the stock persons and the elderly lady there to assist stray customers with the self-checkout machines. Needless to say, the selection was a mite more bounteous than the Walgreen's couple freezer doors—fruits and vegetables galore, a giant organic section, this huge refrigerated beer room that I did my best to avoid walking past, torturous as it was to look at. Unable to have even one beer for fear I'd get a call from the hospital and have to get back in the car. Unable to put on even a slight buzz and take the edge off for just one night.

I could've loaded up on food for the week but only got two or three days' worth. I loved going to the Giant Eagle, found tranquility in having the whole place to myself, in meandering up and down its brightly lit aisles. It was nice being able to do what normal people did without having to do it with them and feel envy and spite.

IV.

That was the extent of my socializing outside the hospital, I should say, for I became even closer to the staff of reSCU than to that of G-53.

Glenn had been in both Iraq and Afghanistan with the army. He was frustrated.

"Over there I was putting in lines, suturing. A doctor, basically. Then I come back and because I don't have the right degree all they'll let me do is trach care and check blood sugar and change linens."

I'd help him and all the aides change Mom's linens and clean her up; that way she didn't have to wait the while it'd take for two of them to be free. And I suppose here's where I'm to comment on how it felt seeing my mother naked, on the impact of getting a good look at that corporeal portal through which I entered the world. Here's where the profundity about the circle of life should go, the bit about your parents changing your diapers and you eventually having to change theirs. But I didn't feel or think anything about it. It wasn't a big deal. She needed cleaning up. I was there and not doing anything. Why not lend a hand?

We had a system, the aides and myself. They draped the bottom sheet over top her, placed the chuck in the center, centered the diaper on that, rolled the whole thing up lengthwise, and set it in one of the chairs. We took away her pillows and I stacked them on the ledge, all six of them: two under her legs, one propping up each arm, one supporting her head, and another behind her back—that one was supposed to be repositioned each hour to keep her off her backside, to further prevent it from breaking down, though it wound up just being every time she was changed, every three or four hours. After we undid the diaper's adhesives and the aide tucked the front of it up underneath her, she was ready to be rolled. The aide lowered the bed flat. I took her under the armpit and helped her toward me. The aide rolled up the old sheet set, diaper and all, till it was up against her back, then went over her with the wipes, put the Xenaderm on her backside and the moisturizer on her back. Meanwhile I brushed her hair, all matted from the pillow. When finished cleaning her, the aide laid the new set on the bed and unrolled it till it was flush with the old one. We switched sides, I helped Mom over the bump and onto her other shoulder, the aide took away the old set and unrolled the rest of the new, we repeated cleaning and combing, laid her back flat, and fastened the new diaper. We each took hold of the new sheet and boosted her up so her head was even with the top of the mattress, then one of us helped her roll toward whatever side she hadn't been on before, the other stuffing the pillow back. Once we'd put back the two beneath her legs—there as much to keep her from sliding down, thin as she was, than to keep her heels off the mattress—the aide raised the bed back up. We put the pillows beneath her arms. I took the last one, changed its case, fluffed it a little, and put it behind her head. If necessary we then changed her gown, the aide took the dirty set away, and that was that.

If only it ever went that smoothly. It was always something—the packet of wipes would turn out to be empty, and while I continued to hold Mom on her side the aide would hurry off to get more; the diaper would be off-center and rather than do it all over again I'd help Mom boost her butt off the bed, almost pick her up, so the aide could slide it over; I'd forget to take the vent hose off the stanchion and when she turned she'd get choked or the nozzle would pop off, sending her into a coughing fit; on days when she'd start having diarrhea, before the cultures were sent off to determine whether it was C. diff and the fecal tube put in, she'd need to be changed as often as every fifteen, twenty minutes.

And yet the aides never complained, *ever,* never lost patience with her or grew even mildly short-tempered. Glenn and another white kid in his mid-twenties were the only two men. The rest were black women ranging in age from their early twenties to one in her seventies. I can't remember hardly any of their names. Not yet, anyway. I'm sure in the months and years to come they'll all sooner or later pop into my head the same way Cheryl's did. On the train one afternoon and all of a sudden, out of nowhere . . . *Cheryl, Mouse, Tank*—the nicknames of her infant grandchildren, both boys, cousins, whose pictures she'd brought in to show off. Can't remember their names but hear all their voices, see all their faces—the girl with the large glasses, the wonderful, high-pitched laugh that makes me smile just thinking of it, and the big afro that she'd sometimes wear in cornrows just as lovely—remember their stories. The girl in her early thirties who, after working all day, had to then go home and care for her own invalid mother. The woman close to Mom's age who'd worked for years in a factory, switching careers after having had to care for her dying father.

If I struggled as child trying to act as parent, with that role reversal, Mom had an even harder time as nurse having to be patient. That's the one thing she wrote in the notebook that stands out above all the rest:

I AM a nurse not were

This to Melanie, no doubt, in frustration over one of the staff referring to her occupation as formerly held. Most of the time the nurses would tell her what they were giving her beforehand, but when they'd forget, she never failed to ask, was constantly inquiring about doses. One nurse, an Asian woman who spoke poor English, Mom didn't care for, and, after putting up with her a couple times, finally asked to see the nurse manager and demanded she be replaced immediately and never assigned to her again. That was the only nurse she had an issue with, however—the rest she had the utmost confidence in and respect for.

I'm better with their names—Samantha; Amy; Jessica; Vicky; Bob; Emily; Day Christina; Night Christina; Jack, who lived all the way in Youngstown, an hour-and-a-half drive each way; Liz, who lived on a farm; Tracy, the best at placing a line; Peter, who spent what precious little downtime there was between call lights sitting in one of the hallway workstation chairs skimming books on personal finance and investment strategy.

Nick was in his mid-thirties, handsome—thin and above average in height with fair skin and slicked-back blond hair. He and his wife had a three-year-old boy. He was remodeling their kitchen himself. A few weeks before we left he'd get his schedule switched to weekends like Stephanie. She was in her early forties. Sandy-blond, shoulder-length hair. Full, rosy cheeks. That voice even more soothing than Dr. Graham's, and the gentlest nature of anyone I've ever met. I'd always let out a sigh of relief upon seeing her walk into the room Friday and Sunday nights. Before doing her assessment— checking blood pressure and pulse, listening by stethoscope to the heart and belly—she'd take Mom's hand and lean in real close and ask how she was feeling. Her father had died of cancer a few years before, had been sick for a long time, and she related to many of my frustrations, answered a lot of my questions, particularly about hospice. The two of us talking in hushed voices while Mom slept—ten, fifteen minutes. She had a toddler and, after getting home from her shift Saturday morning, wouldn't go to bed, would stay up the rest of the day, not wanting to miss a minute. After Mom passed, at the end of that January, a sympathy card came from her in the mail.

It wasn't just the nurses and aides and RTs. I got to be friendly with the housekeeping staff, that floor-obsessed Latino custodian, a few cafeteria servers and cashiers, the two P1 nighttime attendants—the white girl my age on weekdays, on weekends the black woman a little older than Mom who was always reading some trashy romance novel.

Anthony delivered and collected trays for the eighth floor's kitchen. Eighteen or nineteen, he lived in Virginia but was up staying with an aunt and uncle for the summer, curious to see another city. He didn't care for Cleveland, didn't know anybody, and so didn't do much besides work, but was still glad to have come. We talked a lot about his fellow Virginian Michael Vick, whose dog-fighting operation was located in an area Anthony knew well, and he enlightened me on just how prevalent the pastime is there.

As indicated by the mentions of food Mom scribbled in the notebook, they'd tried to get her eating for a little while there when she first got to reSCU. But by the time the Atlanta Falcons quarterback was indicted in mid-July, she was back to just ice chips (and the grape popsicles used by the speech therapist for her swallowing evaluations, the purple liquid rushing into the G-tube just seconds after she'd take a bite). Yet even though he had no tray to bring her, Anthony continued to pop his head in every day and ask how she was. Getting her to smile wasn't easy: When Greg would ask—or the magazine-and-book-cart lady who stopped by each morning, even sometimes Claire if she was feeling especially rotten—Mom would give a sarcastic, toothy one that might as well have been a snarl. She'd always smile for Anthony, though, genuinely, and give him the A-OK sign no matter what. I don't know what was behind their connection, but they clearly had one—"I say a prayer for her every night," he'd tell me—and I found myself wishing he hadn't left to go back home before she'd started getting in the wheelchair, knew he'd have loved to see that.

We didn't have much interaction with the other reSCU families. Except for one woman who was there four or five months—her family bringing in her TV and VCR from home so she could watch videos—the turnover in the unit was fairly frequent: twenty-seven days the average length of stay for 2007. There was one I remember, though.

I'd been so excited that June to watch Oprah's interview with *The Road* author Cormac McCarthy, had gotten to the room early to make sure I didn't miss a second. But that was a bad day, and between emptying her bucket, refreshing her forehead washcloth, and bugging her nurse about getting her Reglan early, I caught only a couple minutes. I did, however, see all of documentarian Michael Moore's appearance on the show a couple weeks later. He was promoting his new movie, *Sicko,* about the state of the country's health-care system— the *deplorable* state, was his contention, and Mom's as well. "There's no excuse," she mouthed, and shook her head during a commercial break. "There's absolutely no reason why everyone shouldn't be covered. It's just not right. It's not. It's unethical." Going on her ninth month of hospitalization, getting arguably the best treatment for her condition in the world, treatment that by then had cost close to a million dollars, if not more, but for which she'd have to pay only that few thousand for the ambulance—wouldn't need to sell the house or dip into her portfolio—yet still railing against the injustice of it all.

I wouldn't need to see Moore's film to know how lucky we were. In late August there'd come into the unit a man in the same shape as Mom when she'd arrived—or so I gathered from what I could see walking past his room. He too had an air mattress and needed both an aide to keep watch and the boots, though he actually wore his. He also seemed to have placed a similar edict on visitors. His wife was the only one I ever saw coming or going. She was in her mid-forties, petite, pale skin and long black hair, usually dressed in sweats or a tracksuit. We never spoke except for the one night I was in one of the waiting-area chairs—Mom's nurse giving me a reprieve from the changing and cleaning.

"Get some rest," the woman said on her way to the elevator.

"You too," I said.

A couple weeks later, maybe a month into their being there, I overheard in the hall a conversation between her and the staff doctor about their insurance. Apparently it'd been refusing to pay for any additional time, but the doctor had fought to secure them a bit more. It was then that I became absolutely certain the case manager's initial push to get us out had nothing to do with money. If so, she'd have told us just that straight—the way Grace's case manager would.

V.

By the time she moved into that infectious-disease room, Mom's foot drop had become so severe that the tops of her feet when in bed were parallel with the mattress—a level plane from ankle to toe. Her left knee, meanwhile, on account of the pillows, had become locked in place, couldn't be fully straightened. Physical therapist Matt ordered these corrective metal boots and knee brace. If worn a little longer each day, with the tension steadily increased—a small wrench was provided for the purpose—eventually the muscles would regain some, though not all, flexibility. When we moved to Grace, having worn the boots and brace more than a month, she'd gotten up to only five hours on the first setting. (Tension wasn't increased until six hours with no pain.) We'd bring them with us—as the insurance had paid for them, they belonged to us, not the Clinic—but Grace's physical therapists didn't think they worked, especially on legs as atrophied as Mom's, so we stopped. Even best-case scenario, Matt had projected the damage would still be significant enough that in order to walk she'd have to wear those shoes with the big Herman Munster heels. She got so mad when she heard that.

"Those things are so ugly," she mouthed.

That was one afternoon before Claire left for the day, and both of us couldn't help but laugh—a good sign she still cared so much about her appearance.

After she'd been on the trach collar a full week and Dr. Daniels had rotated off the floor, I convinced the new staff doctor to let us try taking her outside in a wheelchair. She was a little self-conscious about that, too—even though it was hot, insisted on a sheet across her lap to conceal the G-tube and urine foley bags hooked to the side of the wheelchair—but it was nowhere near enough to stop her. Some days when she was feeling really good she'd make two trips— once with Claire for an hour or so around noon, then with me around seven, while the nurses gave report for shift change. Matt would get her up during the day, but at night I'd be on my own—had a system for that, too.

Once the nurse had disconnected and flushed the Corpak, I got a full oxygen tank from the rack in the hall, slipped it onto the back of the wheelchair (kept in the bathroom), and connected to it the thin, clear plastic tube running to the attachment that fit onto the trach collar. Put the foam pad on the seat and a sheet over top that. Pulled the wheelchair up to the near side of the bed and locked the wheels. Put her socks on. Lowered the bed as far as it'd go so her feet could touch the floor. Put the G-tube and urine foley bags on the floor. Helped her onto her side and then up into a sitting position on the edge of the bed. Let her rest a second. When she was ready, put my left foot between her knees and my right between her and the chair. Made sure to take the tubing connecting the wall oxygen to the trach collar off the stanchion so it didn't yank when we went. On the count of three, with my hands under her armpits, lifted her upright and pivoted, almost danced her around, her on tiptoes because of the foot drop. Eased her into the wheelchair, then used the sheet to scooch her back into the seat. Turned on the tank and switched oxygen sources. Lowered the flaps so she could put her feet up. Sheet, blanket if it was a little cool out, pillow to rest her arms on, paper bucket with four or five tissues inside, another blanket over her shoulders if she wanted.

The first time, her nurse made us promise not to go any farther than the elevators, just to get Mom used to the wheelchair.

"Well?" I asked her when we got there.

"Let's do it," she said, the Passy-Muir on.

I took her down to the F Building lobby, about sprinted us through it, was like a contestant on that old *Supermarket Sweep* game show we both used to love, wanting to get out and back before her nurse got suspicious, get her out there before she started vomiting or feeling short of breath, wanting so bad to just get her out. It'd been almost two months since our detour to radiation.

She waved her hand for me to slow down.

"Making you nauseous?" I asked.

"I want to see it," she said.

All those trips to the T Building she'd been lying flat, staring at the ceiling—this her first chance to really take in the place, her home for the last eleven months.

That night we'd only stay out ten minutes or so, same as the one night a bee wouldn't stop buzzing around her Corpak, attracted by the tube feed's sticky-sweet residue. The night with the Amish guy we weren't even out there *that* long.

He was in his fifties. Beard, straw hat, glasses. Dark-blue pants and vest, light-blue shirt. He came over to us, said, "Nice to be out."

"Yeah," I said. "Nice to get some fresh air."

"Not sure how fresh it is," he said, and looked out at the traffic on Euclid. "But at least it's outside. Out of the hospital."

"Yeah," I said. "Just to get a different view."

He just stood there.

"Do you have a family member here?" I asked him.

"My sister," he said. "She just passed. A couple hours ago."

"I'm sorry," I said. "I'm so sorry."

"There are eleven of us. Six boys. Five girls. She was the youngest."

He stood there quiet. Mom and I just sat there.

"She had leukemia. Some sort of leukemia. Just happened all of a sudden. One night her finger was all swelled up and there were these red marks up her arm. She went to the doctor and doctor said it wasn't anything. Doctor in Mansfield. Then she started getting real sick, so we brought her here. That was August seventeenth. Said it could've been something small she got it from. A little cut. Striking a match, maybe."

"You live in Mansfield?"

"No, a little south of there, near Ashland. Small town. Lot of young kids."

"Yeah, there's the college there."

"Yeah. This your mom?"

"Yeah."

A maintenance guy drove up on a riding mower to cut the little patch of grass by the main entrance's sliding doors. It was loud and hard to hear over. The Amish guy couldn't take his eyes off it.

"It's nice you have all those brothers and sisters for support," I said.

"Yeah," he said. "There's one woman on the floor my sister was. She never had any visitors."

Mom then tapped me on the arm.

"I've gotta go to the bathroom," she said.

"We're gonna head in," I said to the guy and stood up. "I'm so sorry."

"Thanks. Hope she gets out of here soon."

"Thanks. My best to your family."

"You too."

"You gotta go to the bathroom?" I asked her when we got back to the room.

"No."

"You just saying that to get away from the Amish guy?"

"Yeah."

All the other nights we'd stay out forty-five minutes to an hour. Me there on the bench, Mom in the wheelchair beside me, holding hands, feeling the blast of air-conditioning on the backs of our necks every time the doors slid open, watching the people going in and out and the cars and city buses pass, the tall fluorescent lamps on the little plaza and the orange streetlights coming on. Sometimes she dozed off.

I'm a little hesitant to mention this—the going outside. That *Good Soldier* line, the epigraph: I'm writing this more to get it out of my head than for posterity. I have such a hard time remembering her before the hospital. I can if I try, but it doesn't come automatically. In fact, I can't recall a single instance in the two years since she died when I've seen or heard something and it's reminded me of something she did or said, when out of nowhere some comment she made or look she gave popped into my head and I've smiled or laughed. The times I've dreamt of her, even—she's always close to death. Not at the hospice, rather in some strange hospital or sometimes at home, but always me knowing that she's about to go. I don't know why this is, but it's awful.

Yes, to have beheld her courage and defiance, her determination and hope, her faith . . . *privileged* is the closest word there is, but the feeling is far, far greater. And yet it wasn't anything I didn't already know; she proved herself a hero but that's how I always saw her anyway. Granted, I hadn't the faintest idea how great strangers' capacity for kindness and compassion could be. But much as I treasure that awareness, I'd trade it in a second, swap every memory of that fourteen-month odyssey for those that came before. Except our couple dozen or so trips outside—those I cherish as much as any time we ever spent together.

One night I took her across Euclid, to P1 and up to the Corolla so she could get a look at it. That made her happy—she smiled, reached out, and gave it a pat. For a second, I thought to pick her up and put her in and drive away, just get on the road and worry about where to and all the rest of it later. Instead I took her up to the garage's roof, pushed her over to the western wall, and as I massaged her neck and shoulders we looked out at downtown—the Indians at home that night, the lights on at Jacobs Field, the sky a swirl of pink and red and violet.

I took her up there one other time, late the Saturday afternoon of Labor Day weekend. That was also the weekend of the air show, and this enormous, old military transport plane kept circling us—six, seven, eight times—before flying back toward downtown and the airport.

I took her exploring inside the hospital as well—showed her the cafeteria and the only piece of art in the whole place I actually thought worth a damn. (The F Building lobby also served as a gallery, rotating installations as well as paintings.) Located in the small waiting area between the H Building's main reception desk and the chapel, it was a painting of a rickety old slip in some ramshackle harbor town. But three-dimensional and mechanical—the dinghy moored there rocking and swaying, as was a buoy off in the distance whose light blinked. And there were sound effects—the buoy clanging, lapping water, seagulls. She loved it. Fifteen minutes we must've sat there looking.

I also showed her the chapel—tiny, dark, and windowless, with a small marble-slab altar raised a couple steps and two rows of five or six pews separated by a narrow aisle.

I wasn't very spiritual before all this. I kept going to church with Mom for a little while after confirmation, but only because it was better than staying at home watching Robert Schuller's *Hour of Power* with Dad. Once he left, I slept in Sundays, getting more than my fill of dogma during the school week, what with mass every day of obligation in Walsh's own chapel, the requisite theology courses, and electives with such titles as Learning to Live, in which we were cautioned against the perils of substance abuse by watching the movie *Clean and Sober* and listening to Billy Joel's "Captain Jack."

At Tampa I joined the rowing team; we'd shove off the dock by six every morning except Sunday, when I didn't get out of bed till one at the earliest. And Sundays in New York, there was almost always some brunch to be catered. A couple Christmases before the heart attack, I asked for a Bible, having heard that some writer— Cather, I think it was—would read a few pages each day before beginning work. I liked that idea, figuring as the Good Book had so clearly influenced that holy trinity of Hemingway, Faulkner, and Steinbeck, I should become better versed. I gave up at the Table of Nations.

What a year in the hospital will do.

I'd stop in the chapel every night on my way to P1, say an Our Father and a Hail Mary, and write a petition in the notebook on a podium by the door. I'd also say an Our Father and Hail Mary with Mom before leaving the room, her usually asleep from the Ambien before we'd finished. Then, still rubbing her head, I'd say a prayer of my own, under my breath or just in my head. I can still recite it from memory, and once in a while catch myself doing so when saying my nightly prayers:

God, thank you for this day, for giving my mom the strength, the courage, the determination, and the patience to make it through. Please continue to endow her doctors, nurses, respiratory therapists, physical therapists, nurses' aides, and case manager with the wisdom, the determination, and the patience to fix her up and get her home soon. Please continue to keep all of us—her family and friends—healthy in both mind and body so that we may be here to support her as often as possible, to the best of our ability. And in our times of doubt, fear, anxiety, and helplessness, please reaffirm our faith in your grace, your goodness, and your everlasting presence. We thank you, God. We love you. Amen.

Every night, even at hospice—although there I left out the part about fixing her up and getting her home.

CHAPTER TEN

I.

After nearly a month in the infectious-disease room and even longer on the trach collar, she contracted another pneumonia and on September 13 was returned to reSCU proper and placed back on the vent. This time she'd bounce back quick. By October 1 she was off the vent for more than a week and once again able to be capped and talking.

I'm tempted to make up something here about how one afternoon she asked me to switch off the TV, had me turn the high-backed chair to face her, took my hand, and told me it was time, that she was ready to leave and would I make it happen. But it didn't go like that. I don't remember how it went. That first Friday of October, Claire writes that the case manager stopped by to let us know there were no beds currently available at Grace but that we were at the head of the list. But I don't remember having a conversation with the case manager prior to that either way—me instigating it or her once more putting the pressure on and me finally acceding. All I remember is the game that night.

Despite the shellacking of Cliff Lee and, beginning in mid-August, having to play a marathon twenty-three games in as many days to make up for those postponed by the snow in April, the Indians won their first Central Division title since 2001, tying the Boston Red Sox for the best record in all of baseball. Since Boston had the better head-to-head record, though, the Indians were seeded second in the league playoffs and in the opening round drew the Yankees, who'd taken all six regular season meetings between the two clubs.

In the series opener, the Indians scored three runs in the first inning and won 12–3. They should've been more stingy. So it seemed by their turn at bat in the eighth inning of game two, trailing New York 1–0 and now having to face Joba Chamberlain, the rookie set-up man who, thanks to a fastball consistently clocking in the high nineties, had already established himself as one of the majors' most indomitable arms. And it wouldn't get any easier in the ninth; future Hall of Fame closer Mariano Rivera waited in the wings. The next inning and a half were but a formality. The series would be even heading to New York for games three and four.

Then came the bugs.

Midges, to be exact—gnatlike critters that lead a most curious and brief existence. Spawned in large bodies of water—a ten-thousand-square-mile lake named after an Iroquois tribe will do—they fly off in search of a mate the moment they reach adulthood, breed, fly back to lay their eggs, then die—their life span, male and female both, just a few days. Typically, they breed only in summer months, but that night in Cleveland was muggy as all hell, the temperature in the low eighties, and in that bottom frame of the eighth Jacobs

Field, with its megawatt lights and profusion of sweat, suddenly became a dipteran version of the Playboy Mansion.

Play was stopped several times as umpires and Yankee players toweled themselves dry and doused one another with industrial-sized cans of repellant. It didn't help. Shortstop Derek Jeter and the rest of the New York defense waved their gloves in front of their faces, windmilled their arms, and danced around between pitches. Remaining tethered to the pitching rubber and perspiring the most, Chamberlain got the worst of it. The TV close-ups looked like a *Tales from the Crypt* episode, his neck crawling with dozens of the tiny insects.

Chamberlain's temperament was as combustible as his fastball—in an August game against the Red Sox, he'd been ejected after throwing two consecutive pitches over a batter's head—and the swarm unglued him. He walked the first batter of the inning and threw a wild pitch to the next, allowing the runner to advance to second base. A ground-ball out moved him to third and then *another* wild pitch brought him home. Chamberlain would go on to hit a batter and issue his second walk of the inning but manage to get out of it with the score knotted.

On the mound for the Indians, meanwhile, nineteen-game winner Fausto Carmona had thus far been brilliant—the solo home run he'd rendered in the third inning one of only two Yankee hits—and in the top of the ninth he seemed as bolstered by the bugs as his counterpart was unmanned. A native of the Dominican Republic, perhaps he felt more at home. (I'm thinking here of Elaine's stories about visiting her grandmother in Santo Domingo, how her legs would get so swollen from mosquito bites it'd hurt to walk.) Midges covering his face, creeping into his mouth and eyes, Carmona didn't bat a lash as he stared at the catcher for his signs, struck out two, and put up another zero on the left-field JumboTron there above the Cleveland Clinic advertisement. Cleveland's offense couldn't get anything going in the bottom of the ninth, and in the tenth squandered a runner on second base with one out. Yet Carmona's replacement, fellow Dominican Rafael Pérez, was just as dazzling, retiring all six hitters he faced, and in the eleventh the Indians finally prevailed.

Nearly four and a half hours it took. While Mom drifted in and out, I watched every pitch, every aerosol spray, even more astonished than I'd been by LeBron's dismantling of Detroit—less because of the bugs themselves than their benefiting the Tribe.

The Indians couldn't catch a break throughout my childhood and adolescence—nor, for that matter, the majority of the forty-odd years prior to that since their last World Series victory in 1948, particularly following the 1960 trade of home-run king Rocky Colavito, a move most fans believe to have hexed the franchise. Finishing 1987 with the worst record in the majors after *Sports Illustrated* had featured Joe Carter and right fielder Cory Snyder on the cover of that year's baseball preview issue and proclaimed the team American League frontrunners; the deaths of pitchers Steve Olin and Tim Crews in a 1993 spring training boating accident; World Series defeats in 1995 and 1997. That second loss was especially gut-wrenching, coming as it did in the eleventh inning of the seventh and deciding game after having blown a ninth-inning lead. And to, of all teams, the Florida Marlins, in just their fourth year since entering the league under expansion. Four years and Florida with half as many titles as

Cleveland in *ninety-four*. And naturally I just had to be living in Tampa, still a year away from the arrival of the Devil Rays, and so there was no shortage of Marlins commemorative championship gear to have my face rubbed in.

While disowning the Cavs, I continued to follow the Indians—the Browns, too, but because I'd actually played baseball and the Browns were disbanded for three years there in the late nineties, especially the Tribe. I watched them lose the 1998 American League Championship Series and the Divisional Series the following year. I watched the 2000 and 2005 seasons slip by, when they seemed an assured wild-card berth but missed the playoffs by percentage points. And so I should have known that the only way the 2007 campaign could end was in heartbreak, known better after the way the Cavs had been steamrolled by San Antonio than to hitch my hopes for Mom's recovery to the success of *any* sports team, least of all one with a 44115 zip code. It's just those bugs were so bizarre, Carmona's perseverance so inspiring. I couldn't resist taking it as a sign that we were doing right by moving to Grace.

At least that's how I thought I felt. That first day there I'd realize how unsure I really was.

It'd be another two weeks before a bed opened up. When one finally did, the case manager informed us there was a problem with the insurance. They didn't feel Mom's condition warranted an LTAC and would only pay for skilled nursing. I'd always cut the case manager some slack, figuring she'd just been a proxy for Dr. Daniels. But this was inexcusable. Not bothering to check with the insurance

ahead of time. Letting us get our hopes up about Grace, then trying
to cover her ass by making it out like it was a positive, that it meant
Mom was in such shape she could just skip the LTAC.

I knew better. Around the time of the G-and-J-tube procedure
I'd gone ahead and checked out a handful of nursing homes in
Akron. Some were better than others, but by and large they were no
different from what I remembered of Grandma Manning's: that
same stale breath–creamed corn–ammonia smell; at least one poor
kid around my age or younger made quadriplegic in some car or
motorcycle wreck; sad, hand-printed paper nameplates outside the
doors; calendar of activities—bingo, movie night . . . and that being
about it, just bingo and movie night alternating every square; in the
one I looked at with the Alzheimer's wing, the constant yelling and
the nurses saying, "I'm not your wife, dear," or, "The year is 2007."

The nurse-to-patient ratios were eight-to-one, give or take a couple;
they *certainly* wouldn't be able to give Mom the attention she'd need,
suction her as frequently as she'd require—and to do so didn't have
wall units but rather the portable, prehistoric, sewing-machine-
looking versions the Clinic kept around only as last-resort backups.
Furthermore, when her Corpak clogged, an ambulance would have
to be called to take her to the hospital to replace it. Which is to say,
she could expect to be taken to the hospital at least once a month.

At one of them there was this male nurse who gave off a serious
molester vibe—made me want to vomit thinking he'd be changing
her diaper, be alone with her overnight. Another looked familiar
but not until I left did I remember we'd performed there once for
Doo-Wops and Continentals.

Anyway, I finally let the case manager have it. Then I called her
boss and did the same. Like Mom being left stranded in the middle

of G-53 and the trach's shifting, though, the fuck-up actually worked in our favor. The boss leaned on the insurance company, or got the staff doctor to, and the decision was reversed.

That was late in the afternoon of Thursday, October 18, when we found out. Grace didn't accept patients over the weekend, and who knew what might happen given another three or four days in the Clinic—or rather, we knew precisely—so the move would have to take place the very next morning. Though not allowing us to say a proper good-bye to Dr. Graham, the urgency was good in that it didn't give Mom too much time to worry.

Early as I had to be at the hospital, big a day as it'd be, I still stayed as late as ever, waited to leave till she got her Ambien, said our prayer, stopped off at the chapel. Our last night at the Clinic—technically, my second to last.

II.

On the front of the card is a watercolor of two purple hibiscuses. Inside, twenty-two signatures. Close to that many lined both sides of the hall—RTs, aides, nurses. A few even came over from G-80 despite never having taken care of her. All of them clapping.

"Bye, Ms. Manning."

"Good luck, Ms. Manning."

"Be sure to let us know how you're doing."

"Come back and visit."

And the balloon—they also got her a helium balloon in the shape of a butterfly.

This time I was allowed to ride in the ambulance. She'd received some morphine before leaving the room but, on edge as she was, it didn't put her out. It was a rough ride—all that jouncing around, her having to look out the window facing backward, brakes slamming and the ambulance screeching to a halt as we nearly plowed into someone while merging onto westbound I-90. She didn't use it but kept a paper bucket tucked up under her chin the whole way.

Dad drove her car to Fairview so I'd have it. He'd go home with Melanie, who took the afternoon off work, then have a friend drive him to the Clinic in the morning to pick up his car. I'm sure this doesn't seem like a very important detail, but it is when it's you. What to do about the cars, what else to bring in besides the tension boots and knee brace—the fan, corkboard, ducks, lamp despite the base being chipped after getting knocked off the nightstand a few months before, Claire's crucifix. The red Christmas blanket I'd retired long ago, after Mom's first time getting C. diff in reSCU.

It was about twenty minutes before Grace's nurses got her settled and got the heart monitor on and we were able to see her. That was another way besides physical therapy Grace was superior to reSCU: Attached to her chest at all times were a few leads hooked to a battery-powered sensor tucked into her gown's breast pocket, the results transmitted to one of the series of monitors behind the desk of the small nurses' station in the middle of the hall.

She was at the far end, the last room on the right. I'd gotten her all excited about the sight of so many trees, but there was no view of the park, just Lorain Avenue with its shopping plazas and two- and three-story commercial buildings stretching off into the horizon.

"I'm sorry," I said.

"It's nice," she said. "I like it."

Already they'd put on the Passy-Muir, already they were making her work. I broke into tears—one of those rare times I cracked. She smiled—I'll never forget that smile she gave me—and put her arms out. I went to her, bent over, buried my face in her neck and sobbed. She put her arms around me and patted my back.

"I just hope it's the right decision," I said.

"It'll be okay," she said. "It'll be okay."

And that first week it was. The physical and occupational therapists projected she could be walking and dressing herself as early as Thanksgiving. *Thanksgiving! Less than a month!* I started to think maybe the Indians losing as they had hadn't signified anything after all, that there was no corresponding shoe to drop, that that way of thinking was ridiculous, pathological really.

I should have known better.

After finishing off the Yankees, the Indians took a three-games-to-one lead over the Red Sox in the ALCS, only to surrender game five at home as well as game six in Boston. In game seven, also at Fenway Park, the Red Sox scored a run in each of the first three innings while nine of Cleveland's first ten batters failed to reach base. In the fourth, however, the Tribe would get a run back, and another in the fifth.

That was still the score in the top of the seventh, 3–2 Red Sox, when with one out Indians left fielder Kenny Lofton hit what should've been a routine pop-up into shallow left field. Boston shortstop Julio Lugo appeared to have a bead on it and called off incoming left fielder Manny Ramirez, but the ball kicked off his glove and Lofton, the potential tying run, hustled into second base. The next batter up after Lofton, right fielder Franklin Gutierrez, scorched a line drive just fair over third base. The ball hooked into foul ground and ricocheted off the low wall of the photographers' corral back into that same shallow left-field territory where Lugo had booted Lofton's fly. Ramirez raced in from left but was still four or five steps from the ball when Lofton rounded third; to have even an outside chance for a play at the plate would take a clean pickup and exchange and an on-the-money throw, and Ramirez had never been all that sure-handed a defender.

Yet third-base coach Joel Skinner chose not to challenge him, threw up his hands, and halted Lofton at third.

"The ball kicked off hard there and it's hard to tell exactly where it is," Skinner would offer as justification after the game. "I've seen it bounce right back to the shortstop. . . . The ball ended up a little deeper than I thought. But it was one out, runners at first and third. We were okay."

What makes Skinner's apparent failure to consider the possibility of a double play even more incomprehensible is that he played catcher for the laughingstock Indians of the late eighties and early nineties. He'd come to Cleveland from the Yankees in March of 1989, missing the Fumble by a few months. But he'd been in town for the Shot, and as a manager in the Indians' farm system from 1995 until his promotion to third-base coach in 2000 had been a part of the organization throughout its bitter disappointments of the last dozen years. As I was, as were hundreds of thousands of Tribe fans in northeastern Ohio, Joel Skinner should've been banking on that next batter after Gutierrez hitting a ground ball were Lofton to remain moored at third.

That's what happened. The Red Sox turned two to get out of the inning and maintain the lead, in the bottom half extended it to three runs, and tacked on six more in the eighth. Final score: Boston 11,

Cleveland 2. In the World Series, the Red Sox would sweep the Colorado Rockies.

"You have to make a decision," Skinner said. "And that's what I did."

What Grace did, too. In the end, it'd turn out to make not a damn bit of difference. Even if Mom had remained free of the vent, continued to progress with the physical therapy, she still wouldn't have been strong enough for chemo. The cancer still would've gotten her. Actually, it was probably better, working as hard as she was there at the very end—spared her further physical anguish and, along with the rest of us, even greater disappointment. But the decision to start with the fluids that Sunday—a week to the day of game seven—seemed just then as rally-killing, as damning to defeat as what has since come to be known as the Stop Sign.

Unlike with Skinner, though, I had no right to be mad. I *was*—fucking pissed—but hadn't the right. Grace was nowhere near as familiar with Mom's history as Skinner should've been with the Indians', with the accursedness of Cleveland sports in general. It'd taken reSCU's nurses, after all, six, seven months to get the blood-pressure balancing act down, to know exactly when to start and stop the fluids. Couldn't expect Grace's to in a week. And as they were just as unfamiliar with me, with my knowledge of her history, I couldn't expect them to think I knew what I was talking about, to be listened to when Sunday night, after a full bag, and then a second—the edema getting really bad, her heart rate in the low 130s—I pleaded for Lasix. Probably to shut me up more than anything, her nurse finally called the doctor and got a onetime dose. But that'd be it—that next day, although the fluid stopped, no order for the diuretic, wanting that blood pressure kept up, and so her still all puffed-up and short of breath. Amazing, really, that she lasted all of Monday and through the night on her own—sheer will.

Tuesday morning she went back on the vent. The next day was Halloween.

"Remember that time with the pumpkin?" I asked her that afternoon.

I was in fourth grade, watching TV in the living room. Mom was in the kitchen starting dinner. Through the picture window I saw this older kid, an eighth or ninth grader, come walking across the yard. I figured he was collecting *Beacon-Journal* subscription money, but instead of ringing the doorbell, he picked the pumpkin we'd carved up off the flower box, slammed it on the concrete porch, and took off running.

"Mom!" I yelled. "The paperboy just smashed the pumpkin!"

She came out of the kitchen wondering what the hell I was talking about. I showed her out the window.

"Which way'd he go?" she asked.

I pointed.

"Keep away from the stove," she said, then grabbed her keys, jumped into her car, and zoomed out the drive.

Not a minute later Dad pulled in from work. After I told him what happened—". . . spiked it just like Ickey Woods!"—he hauled out the trash can and, still in his dress shirt and tie, started cleaning up the pulpy mess. Just as he was finishing, Mom pulled in with the kid in the passenger seat, humiliation on his face.

"Jim!" she yelled as they got out. She was furious. "I wanted *him* to do that."

"I got it," Dad said.

"You got lucky," she told the kid. "Go on."

He mumbled an apology, stuffed his hands in his pockets, and, chin to his chest, shambled off.

At my mention of it, Mom smiled and shook her head.

"Your dad," she mouthed. "Lucky I wasn't arrested for kidnapping."

She was disconsolate about being back on the vent but not nearly as much as the other times. Probably figured it'd be just like the last, that she'd come right off again.

III.

The near-hour drive to Fairview and Grace was like being in a NASCAR race—90 with its four lanes each way, the slowest moving at seventy, cars jockeying for position. Most dangerous were Sunday afternoons following Browns home games. The fleet of Day-Glo orange RVs and shitbeater school buses swerving all over the road, their drivers' vision impaired by rubber dog masks, reaction time slowed from tailgating since dawn—although less drunk, no doubt, than they'd been, than they'd *had* to be throughout the previous four seasons, when the team went an abysmal 19–45.

The Browns would finish 10–6 in 2007 but, of course, *still* fail to make the playoffs after tying for the last spot with the Tennessee Titans, who had a better record against shared opponents; I can only imagine how hard I'd have taken *that* were Mom to have lived long enough. With six players named to the Pro Bowl, they were certainly a talented enough team to compile such a record. But they also had a good deal of luck, no more so than on November 18, when they played the Ravens in Baltimore.

As time expired, Browns kicker Phil Dawson attempted a fifty-one-yard field goal that would've tied the game and sent it to over-time, but the ball bounced off the crossbar, was ruled no good, and the Ravens ran into their locker room to celebrate. A few minutes later they were called back onto the field. The referees had reviewed the field goal and determined the ball had hit not the crossbar but the curved support post, technically beyond the uprights and there-fore good. The game went to sudden death after all. Cleveland won. I still hadn't learned my lesson.

When have we ever gotten a call like that?! Seriously, something's going on.

Actually, around that time things *did* start looking up—compared to those three weeks since she'd been put back on the vent, anyway. First it'd been the Corpak, then the C. diff, then the UTI (the pain so bad she needed morphine). Before leaving reSCU, she'd received a peripherally inserted central catheter (or PICC), a more permanent central line less prone to infection—supposed to be, anyway; one was tried earlier in reSCU but only lasted a few days—and place-able in the arm rather than the neck, chest, or thigh. But it started acting up and would only work with her arm angled a certain way. She became septic. The longest she was able to last off the vent was two hours. She was only strong enough to sit in the chair for one and in bed struggled to get through her half hour's worth of stretch-ing and strength exercises with PT and OT. The nausea. The vom-iting.

After Dawson's kick, though, things settled down. She wasn't walking on Thanksgiving, damn sure wasn't dressing herself, but by that following Monday she'd gotten up to ten hours off the vent. And when Claire showed up that Tuesday morning, she found the room empty—Mom taken by wheelchair down the hall to the PT room for an hour-long session. When she returned to her room, she asked to sit in the chair and stayed there an additional hour.

But was she really feeling better? Or was she just gutting it out, knowing what was at stake, the consequence of not showing some improvement soon?

Our month was up November 19, but since that week was Thanksgiving, the insurance company agreed to another week before deciding her fate. More so that it wouldn't interfere with their vacation plans, I suspect, than out of any holiday kindness. I suspect they'd already made up their minds. For despite the recent upswing, Grace's case manager informed me the provider had once again ruled that Mom stood to benefit no more from an LTAC than from skilled nursing and would henceforth only cover the latter.

I'd expected this—it was why the previous week I'd made an appointment for that Wednesday morning to see my old CYO coach, one of northeastern Ohio's most prominent criminal-defense attorneys.

It'd been fifteen years since I'd last seen him, pacing the St. V sideline, beseeching the refs to blow their whistles and us to box out as vehemently as he would jurors to acquit. He looked in great shape, as if he could still get up and down the court showing how to run the break or break the press, and cut as distinguished a figure as I remembered—full head of thick black hair, trust-effecting eyes, warm smile that put one instantly at ease.

Busy as he was, he had his secretary schedule me in right away. We sat in his Main Street office and caught up—him behind an immense desk free of clutter and me in a chair in front, the large room filled with the light of the cold, clear day as it streamed in through the big unshaded windows. His youngest son had been our point guard and leading scorer, always got his name in the *Beacon-Journal*. He now worked in sales or marketing for some Cleveland company, Coach said. I told of what I'd been doing and updated him on the couple guys from the team I still kept in touch with.

Then Coach took out a yellow legal pad and uncapped a pen. Fifteen, twenty minutes I talked, without a single interruption from him. He made a few notes but mostly just sat there listening. It was the first time I'd ever run it all down for anybody from the beginning. It was the first time I realized the extent of the hell Mom had been through. Perhaps that's why Coach agreed to see me. Perhaps he figured talking to someone relatively objective might do me some good, help me gain a little perspective or at least just give me the chance to let off some steam. I also realized this wasn't what she would've wanted, me looking for someone to sue, anyone, any way to get enough money so that we wouldn't have to rely on the insurance and could just pay for the LTAC or anything else that might better her chances ourselves. Actually, I'd kind of figured that already—it was why I hadn't told her about the meeting, first wanting to find out from Coach what our options were.

He didn't think we had any, really. With someone in such critical condition, and doctors without time to properly weigh options, having to make split-second decisions, it's near impossible to prove liability. Even if you could, there was a statute of limitations to bringing a suit, a year I think it was, and we'd passed it. And anyway, it'd be a long time before we could even think about seeing any money—before we could even *think* about thinking about it.

Nevertheless, he said he'd share it all with a malpractice associate, and if the guy thought it worth pursuing he'd be in touch. He never was. I never told Mom about the meeting.

That same afternoon at Grace I asked the case manager for the corporation president's name and number. I wanted to see if he would, in fact, let us pay ourselves. Mom had close to a hundred thousand dollars in investments—annuities, IRAs, and so forth, which typically can be withdrawn without a penalty if used toward medical expenses. I wasn't considering selling the house—getting back there was one of the biggest things driving her—but if it came to that, we could get at least another hundred twenty.

Before making the call, though, I asked if they might do a scan, either CT or PET, to check on the cancer. In case there's no point in doing the move to skilled nursing was how I put it. I didn't actually believe that'd be the case. I just figured, they do the scan on Thursday, get the results back Friday, can't do anything over the weekend—that'd give her another four days to wean, maybe get up to a full twenty-four hours off the vent. The better she was doing, the stronger my case to make to the president. As with suggesting the G- and J-tubes to Dr. Daniels, I only wanted time.

Just as when I'd seen Dr. Martin's face that night in G-53, I knew as soon as I saw the hospital's number on my caller ID that Friday morning. It was the doctor—his name and physical description not important, for that's all he was to me now, just another doctor, one more bearer of bad news. The cancer had spread to her liver; the scan had shown a mass so large there was no need for a biopsy. There was no way it could be treated, certainly not in her condition. The hospice coordinator wouldn't be in that afternoon; I'd have to wait to meet with her Monday. The doctor thought it best not to tell Mom till then, till the arrangements were made. That way she didn't have to sit with it all weekend.

He gave me the name and number of the Fairview oncologist he'd consulted, in case I had any questions. I called him right away. He assured me there was no possible treatment. I still didn't want to believe it. I called Dr. Graham and left a message with his secretary. He called me back later that afternoon as I was driving up. I told him the news. He confirmed what I'd been told, that unruffled voice I'd gained such an appreciation for over all those months full of sadness.

What made it all worse was what I found upon arriving in the unit. There she was in the hallway, just about even with the nurses' station, a physical therapist to either side holding her up, her left foot on tiptoe, her face a grimace of pure agony. But, still, walking.

At least with the first discovery of the tumor she'd been unconscious most of the time. Watching her struggle to breathe all weekend and encouraging her as always that she could do it, *must* do it, having to pretend that it mattered. It was awful. I don't know what else to say about it.

IV.

Monday I came in early to meet with the hospice coordinator. Just as the case manager at the Main Campus wasn't permitted to suggest an LTAC, this woman couldn't recommend a hospice. I didn't need her to. There was only one in Akron, the one where Claire volunteered, and I wanted her back there. She belonged back there. She was born in Akron. She should die in Akron. What I really wanted was to do it at home, but after making it up to sixteen hours off the vent, she'd cracked that same morning and had to be put back on. Between that and the Corpak, it'd be too difficult.

Also, in Akron it'd be easier for people to visit. I had this idea that once she got over the initial shock she'd come to terms with it, and imagined those last days, well, not as a party but at least the ban on visitors lifted, an endless stream of family and friends coming to reminisce, crying some, but laughing more. According to the hospice coordinator, there was no saying how long she might live. It might be a few days. It might be a month or more. It was only three weeks till Christmas. I saw us watching *A Christmas Story* one last time.

Claire stuck around. Roger was in town and he came up, too. Dad didn't, fearing he'd break down and only make things worse. The doctor came in a little after six. Roger was standing to her left, Claire to her right. I stood at the foot of the bed next to the doctor. He told her. Instantly she started crying. The look on her face, in her eyes.

Later, after she was gone, Dad and I got into a huge shouting match, the biggest argument we'd ever gotten into. Now when I think about what started it I have to laugh. I think Mom would, too. He'd decided to start dating again, and when I stopped over this one afternoon he asked me to take a picture of him that he could post on match.com or eHarmony or whatever. We went out to the backyard for more light and I took four or five with his digital camera, but he wasn't happy with any of them. I took it personally and gave him some attitude, and when he asked what my problem was, I told him how I couldn't believe he'd ask me to do that just a few months after Mom dying.

"You could've just said no."

"It's the fact you'd even ask."

It escalated from there. All that bullshit time and distance had supposedly helped me get over? Yeah, not really. But the divorce wasn't what it was about. To get to *that* took another forty-five minutes. By then we'd moved back inside. It was getting dark but we hadn't turned on any lights. I sat in one of the armchairs, Dad on the couch. I just cried and cried, and every time I'd try to say it, the tears would just keep coming and stop me. Finally I managed.

"I just think about that look in her eyes. How scared she was. Here's this woman who had so much faith and she was just terrified. It'd have been one thing if one of the infections did it or another heart attack. If it could've happened just like that, without her knowing. But after everything she went through, as much as she suffered, to have to then hear that, experience that fear. It's just awful. It's fucking awful. I just don't understand."

The doctor left. Claire was leaning close, on her knees practically, holding her hand. Roger stood there rubbing her head. Both of them saying anything they could think of that might comfort her. She didn't hear them. Neither did I. "I love you," I kept mouthing over and over while we looked at each other and cried. "I love you so much." Finally I went to her, squeezed in front of Roger. It wasn't like the birthday hug that night before the G-and-J-tube procedure. I wasn't delicate about it. I wrapped my arms around her, lifted her up off the bed and held her tight.

Claire still made a journal entry for that day—at least started to. A couple lines in she stops midsentence, as if only then realizing the pointlessness. The rest of the marble composition book—the second of two—is blank.

It should be *sign the paper*, not *pull the plug*. Sure, there were the power cords to the vent and the pulsox. But in order for those to be yanked, I first had to sign the "Do Not Resuscitate" paper—the DNR.

I was reluctant at first, out there in the hall with the hospice coordinator, the two of us standing before the little flip-down writing surface that held Mom's binder. (By the end of her time at the Main Campus, she'd filled up three and was halfway through a fourth.) I wasn't scared of the responsibility. In fact, I insisted on being the one, wouldn't think of asking Claire. I had learned to do the things that need doing and would do whatever those might be till the end. No, I resisted because I didn't want her dying till she got to Akron. None of the hospice's couple dozen beds were open and there was no saying when one would be. I'd figured she could be left on the vent until the move, but it didn't work like that. The coordinator couldn't begin making arrangements until the paper was signed. And the more I delayed, the further down the list she dropped.

So at last I took the pen. I signed my name.

With that, the vent and the pulsox were removed from the room—to make easier the psychological transition to the "comfort care" status Dr. Waters had described, the adjustment to the idea that the numbers were no longer of any importance. I took the pulsox's disappearance the hardest, as again I'd never made any sense of the vent settings, never much bothered to look. The pulsox, though, I'd been glancing at, one or another, at least every thirty seconds for over a year, checking her heart rate and sats. In the days before she was transferred to hospice, I'd still catch myself doing it, only to find empty the nightstand by the window where the monitor had been.

She was now also able to receive morphine on demand. And demand it she did. "Put me out," she mouthed after Roger and Claire had left and we'd cried a bit longer. "Just put me out." After that, every time she'd come to, it was the first thing she'd ask for, until I learned to tell when it was starting to wear off and asked the nurse myself.

I stayed with her every night that week. Claire still came mornings—except Friday, when Dad came to drive the car back so I could ride in the ambulance—and I'd go home and shower and get a couple hours' sleep. But that's all the rest I'd get. I couldn't sleep in the room. I didn't want to. I figured I'd catch up later, after. I just sat in the chair and watched TV and held her hand. Always holding her hand or rubbing her feet. Never wanting to stop touching her so long as I still could.

*　*　*

The ambulance was supposed to have been there around one o'clock Friday afternoon but got delayed till a little before five. Luckily.

Still another thing Grace had going for it over reSCU, I'd come to realize, was its tube feed pump. Along with the feed, there was hooked up a bag of water, and every fifteen minutes or so the Corpak would be flushed automatically. I called the coordinator at the hospice to see if they might be able to get us one. She'd had no idea we'd needed a pump, hadn't been told Mom had a feeding tube. It didn't keep her from being admitted—they had little experience with feeding-tube patients, but got one every now and then. And the woman knew the type of pump; she'd be able to get it. But she wanted to make clear I understood that if the Corpak did clog, that'd be it. They'd stop feeding, take it out. I told her I did and was okay with that.

The ambulance delay got us stuck in going-home traffic, bumper-to-bumper on southbound 77. They didn't use the sirens. By the time we got there it was dark and the morphine she'd been given before leaving Grace had worn off. She was wide awake—those few feet the gurney traveled from the ambulance to the patient entrance the last time she'd ever be outside.

Claire was there to meet us. She went with Mom into her room, and while the nurses got her situated, Dad and I sat at the table in the kitchen area with the coordinator and I signed some more papers. All along the counters were plates of cookies and brownies and Rice Krispies treats brought in by the other patients' families. During the days, along with the sweets, there'd be set out ham and casserole and rolls and other food provided by some church.

Claire had always said how nice the place was, and though I trusted her, though there wasn't any alternative if it hadn't been, I'd visited earlier in the week to see for myself and found she'd actually undersold it. The minute I walked in I felt at peace. Before that, even, pulling into the parking lot—the one-story, tan-brick, many-windowed building well set back from the road on sixteen mildly wooded acres laid out with gardens, stone paths and gazebos, creeks and ponds and a private lake. Inside the lighting was warm, the window and door casings and many of the walls richly colored wood. There were several sitting rooms throughout, the largest with a twenty-foot-high ceiling, wall-to-wall bookshelves, and a grand piano, although I never heard it played. I never heard anything. It was so quiet.

The rooms were located along three hallways extending off the large hub of a nurses' station. Each was big, about twice the size of her bedroom at home, with a full-sized, adjustable (though not in-flatable) bed; full bath; oversized armchair that folded out into a cot; mahogany entertainment center housing a TV slightly bigger than those at the Main Campus and Grace; round cherrywood writing table and two matching chairs; nightstand; two or three lamps; and French doors that opened outside onto one of the paths and provided a good amount of natural light. A three-star hotel room—the tube feed pump and the wall suction unit with secretion canister the only medical equipment.

When I finally finished the paperwork and Dad and I got back to see her, she was propped up in bed, wearing a clean gown, hair combed, bright-eyed and smiling.

"It's so nice," she mouthed.

Was it all the morphine? Delirium brought on by oxygen deprivation? Did she know where she was? I didn't think of these things at the time. I was just so happy to see her smiling, to have her back close to home.

Those are the last words I remember her saying to me. And except for when I was struggling to unclog the Corpak, the last time I'd ever see her awake.

V.

Around eleven Saturday night the tube feed pump started alarming. For ten minutes or so the nurse tried flushing it using one of the big, 60-cc syringes, but the clog wouldn't budge. She let me try, brought me some ginger ale, and for the next hour I stood there drawing back, pushing, drawing back, pushing. Once I forced it too much and the ginger ale sprayed all over my shirt and the wall behind the bed and Mom's face. It wasn't that which caused her eyes to open but me drying her off with a towel.

"It's okay," I said. "The stupid tube feed's just acting up. I'm just trying to fix it."

She drifted right back off.

When the nurse returned to see if I was having any luck, I asked if they had any Clog Zapper.

"It's like this white paste. Comes in these little packets. It pretty much always works."

She'd never heard of it.

I knew I should just let it go. There would be no laughing, no Christmas. *No good, no happiness could come out of this now, so the quicker it was over the better.* But I couldn't—I just couldn't bear the thought that she'd be starving to death.

In my wallet I still had one of Dr. Graham's cards he'd left on the tray table. I called the Clinic's main number, asked to be connected to G-81, and asked the receptionist there if I could speak with Nick. He was off the floor, so I left my name and number. Twenty minutes later he called back.

"I wasn't sure you'd recognize the name," I said.

"Of course," he said. "What's going on?"

I asked if it'd get him in any trouble.

"Nah," he said. "But rather than drive all that way, first, if you can find some, try meat tenderizer. That works just as good."

Giant Eagle was only a five-minute drive. As I checked myself out, the elderly lady was explaining to a group of guys at the next self-service checkout that the store didn't sell beer past twelve.

Mixed with water, the tenderizer loosened the clog a little but not enough. I called Nick back on his cell and told him to expect me soon.

The drive took an hour and a half. It'd been raining all night. With the cold the roads were really icy. There was hardly any traffic—I saw maybe three other cars heading north—but I still took it slow. After a week of almost no sleep, I started to drift off a couple times and so cranked the radio and rolled all the windows down.

It was close to three when I got up to the unit. Vicky and Emily and a couple of the aides were working. Nick must've told them I was coming. They didn't act the least bit surprised to see me, and out of respect didn't ask what had happened since we'd left. I told them anyway—it was the least I owed them—and they all said how sorry they were.

Nick gave me the packet of Clog Zapper and walked me to the elevator. We talked a little about how he was in the doghouse with his wife for still not having finished the kitchen.

The work on the new heart center appeared to be proceeding just as ploddingly, and wouldn't be completed till September of the following year. (I always thought it'd be interesting to see photos of where the construction had been when we arrived compared to when we left.) But since my last time there, new tollbooths had been put in P1. And they were no longer left unstaffed after midnight. That'd been the one benefit to leaving as late as I would—I'd push the button to contact security and they'd lift the gate remotely, saving me a booklet ticket. That night, though, the weekend lady was still there, reading one of her bodice rippers.

"You still working here?" she asked as I paid.

"No," I said. "Not anymore. I just dropped by to say hi to some old coworkers."

The Clog Zapper did a good job, but not good enough. I gave up about five. That afternoon one of the nurses would pull out the Corpak. Mom wouldn't flinch, wouldn't even know.

Dad had an artificial tree. We set it up and strung it with white lights. We'd leave it there for the next person.

Claire would show up around nine. I'd be back by two or three. The rest of the afternoon and evening family would come in and out—Roger and Alice, Andrea and Jeff, Julia's kids and their spouses, Melanie and Sully. Mom hadn't said anything about having visitors either way, but I knew she wouldn't want to be alone. Plus, now that I could afford to think about other people, I realized how everybody had their own relationship with her and how important it was to them to be there.

By nine or ten at night everyone would have gone and it'd be just Dad and me, taking turns brushing her hair while the other rubbed her feet or just sat in the armchair holding her hand. He'd leave around eleven. I'd walk him out and go into the sitting room with the piano and call Elaine. After we'd talked for a few minutes—*she'd* talked—I'd go back, get sheets out of the linen closet across the hall, and make up the cot. I'd stand at the side of the bed and say our prayer while rubbing her head. I'd kiss her forehead and tell her I loved her. I'd lie down and watch TV—Nick at Nite, *The Fresh Prince*.

I brought in her blanket from home, the one I'd found balled up in the chair on that first visit to the house. Powder blue, it had SUSIE stitched big in white in one of the corners. A gift from someone—I can't remember who. I folded it in thirds and, with the name showing, draped it across her legs.

Monday I'd just gotten home and out of the shower when Claire called.

"Better get back," she said. "Her nurse doesn't think it'll be much longer."

I threw on some clothes and raced over.

The nurse apologized when she came on the next morning.

"Sometimes they surprise you," she said.

* * *

One afternoon a gospel choir came through the halls caroling. I was the only one in the room at the time. When they reached us they were singing "Silent Night." I wept.

Lying on my left side, I'd reach up with my right hand and hold hers until my arm started going numb. Then I'd roll onto my back and use my left.

One afternoon—that same afternoon as the choir?—I went out to get lunch. When I came back was when the St. V priest was doing the anointing. He was just finishing—himself, Claire, Roger and Alice, and a couple of Julia's kids gathered around the bed. I wasn't upset nobody had thought to wait or at least call. I didn't want to see that, to be in that little circle.

Each night she became more and more congested, her breathing more and more gurgly. A rattle is right—and loud. It got so that I was asking the nurse to suction at least once an hour. I wasn't sure if it made any difference to Mom or not, but I had the nurse do it anyway just in case.

The nurse touches my shoulder. I'd drifted off. My hand had come away.

"Honey," she says. "She's gone."

"Okay," I say.

"Just let me know when you're ready for me," she says, then leaves and shuts the door.

I get up, turn off the TV. I go to the side of the bed. I lean down and kiss her on the lips and tell her I love her. I kneel and say a prayer and cry.

Next door there's a small sitting room, the very last room on our side of the hall. I go in there and call Dad, Melanie, Claire. Claire says she'll call Roger. I call Elaine. She'll get the soonest flight she can.

It's just before six, maybe a couple minutes past. The two walls making up that corner of the building are each a lattice of a half dozen rectangular windows. Beyond, one of the paths winds through one of the gardens, now dormant. Off in the distance, a forest of broadleaf trees, limbs bare. It's just light enough I can see them.

I.

It was so much easier than it could've been, than it is for so many—
Anne at General, Julia's niece setting us up with Dr. Martin, Melanie handling things at work, Jeff. In his case, not just easier but
more humane, more meaningful. That it was him rather than some
stranger who came to pick up the body, who'd bring her ashes to the
cemetery for interment a couple weeks later. Him in the funeral-
home basement going over the details with me and showing where
to sign, us sitting at the same table Elaine would lay out during calling hours with crudités and charcuterie and bread for sandwiches—
except for some of the soda and beer, which we'd use the next day
for the get-together at Dad's after the funeral, all of it cleaned out
by night's end.

No thanks to me. I didn't want any, wasn't hungry, but also didn't
have the chance. From a few minutes before five right up until nine
it was one person after another—hadn't shaken so many hands since
Sully and I ran for office: his parents; a half dozen neighbors; the
whole family, of course; Sully himself—just off work and still in
uniform—along with Ben and the rest of the Walsh guys; a couple

of those girls from Social Security she'd go to dinner with; Melanie and the rest of the nurses from the health department in addition to their boss—not only of the clinic but the entire department.

"That was a big deal," Melanie told me later. "He doesn't come out unless it's for something really important."

"Your mother was great at her job," he said after introducing himself and offering his condolences. "Just a terrific, terrific nurse."

How much that would've meant to her!

That was why we'd chosen—Claire and I, going through her closet the afternoon before—a light-blue turtleneck and navy pants: Her work dress code was white or some shade of blue. It had to be a turtleneck because of the stoma.

She had too much makeup on. When I'd first got there Claire was trying to wipe off some of the lipstick with a tissue. She was upset about it. It didn't bother me, probably because it made her look less like herself, the whole thing less real. The tissue only made it worse. The lipstick flaked off and smeared her cheek a little. Claire was able to wipe the smear off but quit after that.

"I tried, sister," she said, and patted Mom's clasped hands. They clutched the rosary that hung from the crucifix in her bedroom. She wore diamond earrings and the necklace she'd had on that day of the heart attack, the one I'd gotten her a few Christmases ago.

As for me, knowing it was what she'd have wanted, hearing her in my head say, "Oh, sure, *now* you listen to me, when I don't even get to see it," after I picked Elaine up at the airport we went straight to the mall and I bought a brown sweater and tan dress pants along with a suit for the funeral. After Mom being on me all summer to "cut that ratty hair"—at its longest, it reached my chin—I'd finally yielded once at Grace, buzzed it all off just as I'd done to appease my catering bosses a week or so before the heart attack.

They and the waiters and chefs had sent flowers. So had the health-department nurses, Claire's girlfriends. Dad's side of the family. There were about a dozen arrangements total. Things were so crazy I didn't get a chance to look at them till we were getting ready to leave. Dad himself had sent one. SEE YOU SOON, the card read. That was the only time I cried all night.

II.

Sitting there in that 140-year-old church with the brass push clasps on the backs of the pews once used by Grandpa Hesidence and the rest of the men to hold their hats. The marble stoups and carved Stations of the Cross. How hot it'd get in the summer without any air-conditioning—the ceiling fans going full speed and the bottom portions of the stained-glass windows opened but doing little good, everyone fanning themselves with the bulletin. The white envelopes for offerings to the poor she used to give me to color on. The dollars she'd hand me to put in the basket—how we'd always friendly bet on what reserve bank they'd come from.

I read Tennyson's "The Deserted House."

Come away: for Life and Thought
Here no longer dwell;
But in a city glorious—
A great and distant city—have bought
A mansion incorruptible.

I held Elaine's hand.

I didn't cry.

The sky was gray.

III.

The day of the interment was overcast as well.

The plot was on top of a small but steep rise. The ground was muddy and slick. Roger led the way, Jeff behind him carrying the square, marble urn. I took Claire's and Alice's arms while Dad helped Melanie and Andrea. The footing was so bad we were forced to step on others' markers.

Grandma's was covered in leaves. Roger bent over and brushed them off. A waist-high wooden stand was set up on a large green mat. Jeff placed the urn on it, then made the sign of the cross and bowed his head; the priest was sick with food poisoning, so Jeff delivered the rites. Dad, Roger, and Claire said them along. I'd been to enough funerals that the ancient words should've sounded at least a little familiar. They didn't. They sounded mysterious and menacing but also beautiful in a way. *We are dust and unto dust we shall return.* The same as all those headstones spread out everywhere, as far as the eye could see—kind of beautiful, but mostly terrifying.

Back at the cars, Jeff gave me a shopping bag full of stuff from the calling hours—the guest book, her jewelry. I put the bag in the car, then ran back up the hill. I put my fingers to my lips and placed them on the urn.

"Love you, Mom," I said, and crossed myself one last time.

A couple hundred yards down the narrow lane was another procession. There were a few elderly men in uniform holding rifles. They fired a couple shots. The echo lingered on the cold, still air.

Dad, Jeff, and Melanie had to get back to work. The rest of us went to the mausoleum to see Uncle Max. Next to his slot in the wall was one reserved for Claire, standing right there beside me.

Driving toward the gate, I glanced once more in the direction of the grave. Directly above, the sun had poked out.

IV.

Dad knew how eager I was to get back to New York—was himself eager to see me go, to return to my old life. (He now admits he knew how difficult this would be but that it'd have been even harder the longer I stuck around.) So along with selling the Corolla, he offered to handle putting the house up. All I'd have to do was clean it out.

There was plenty to do before I could begin. Meet with Mom's lawyer and sign all the probate papers to get the car and house transferred. Have the appraiser over. Close her checking account. Pick up her life-insurance check downtown at the city payroll office. Pay the funeral home. Fill out and send in the paperwork to get the remainder of her pension—and, having missed a line and getting it returned in the mail, send it in again. Forward the mail to Dad's. Meet with her financial adviser to transfer her investments and find out what exactly a mutual fund was now that I had some.

For nearly everything I needed to provide a death certificate—even just to cancel the cable, the landline, finally her cell; I ran out and had Jeff order me a few more. And with the holidays, all of it took longer. I didn't start cleaning till early February.

It was never ending. Box up the china and silver and crystal. Toss the everyday dishes and glasses and utensils plus what little food was in the fridge and cupboards. Bundle for recycling the phone books and cookbooks and her old nursing-school texts she'd kept for reference. Take the old pickle jars and margarine containers full of change to the Acme's counting machine. Drop off the bags of clothes at Goodwill. With Sully's help, lug whatever furniture I didn't want down to the garage with the rest of the trash so Dad could just hire somebody to haul it all away. There were thirty bags, easy. The garage got so full there wasn't any room to pull the car in.

Had I stayed focused, I could've been gone by the end of the month. Sidetracked as I kept getting, it was closer to April.

The videotapes, for instance. There must've been thirty, forty. Most were old *Oprah*s or Masters, but I still fast-forwarded through every one from start to finish. It was worth it. I found footage of the two of us at Virginia Beach when I was six or seven, on vacation with one of the Social Security girls and her son my same age. Me racing the tide and tripping, losing a sandal, it getting sucked back out and me standing there scared to go in after it, looking back at her for help and her behind the camera yelling, "Well, go on! Go get it before you lose it!"

There were the sports cards I'd thrown on the shelf of my bedroom closet when I was eleven or twelve and hadn't looked at since. I'd forgotten I had so many. There was a giant square cardboard box and another rectangular one plus three big binders full of commons. I had to laugh at what a little control freak I'd been—had them all separated by brand and in numerical order. My rares I kept in hard cases in this red plastic pencil box from grade school. At least they were rares when I put them in there—Alex Cole, Jeff

George, Sherman Douglas. Probably the only one still worth anything was the Ken Griffey Jr. rookie from that first Upper Deck complete set.

In the utility room I found our first-ever answering machine. Using the recorder from the meeting with Drs. Graham and Waters, I was able to play the tape. Mostly it was just beeps and hang-ups, but mixed in were a few messages—one from Dad at work asking to pick up if anyone was home, another from cousin Andrea inviting Mom to lunch, one from Tanya.

She was this girl with bulletproof-thick bifocals and a Jheri curl in Litchfield's Specific Learning Disability class. I'd never talked to her before, ever, but one day she decided I was her boyfriend and called every night for three weeks. I don't know how she got my number. The first week or so, Mom was real nice about it. I'd be standing there shaking my head and giving her the throat-slash sign, and she'd tell Tanya real sweet and patient I wasn't home. By the end of the third week, she told Tanya she would be speaking with the principal if the calls didn't stop. Next day I got dumped and Tanya started going out with Ben.

I called him and played the tape into the phone. He guessed who it was right away. He'd gotten it even worse than me. A whole month she'd called him.

In the garage I found my old skateboard. I took it for a couple turns around the neighborhood. I nearly broke my neck and got heckled by some kids.

I waited to do her room last. Claire came over and helped with the clothes, separated everything into three piles: stuff she wanted for herself, stuff for Goodwill, and stuff to get trashed. Along with those old Social Security papers, we found in the closet a box with her wedding dress, another with some of my old baby clothes, and one full of photos I'd never seen. Pictures of the honeymoon—one of Mom in red bell-bottoms with her hair halfway down her back standing in front of some stone wall next to a cannon. An Olan Mills one of the three of us from when I was about a year old. Dad in a mustache and suit and still a little hair attempting to look all dignified while clinging onto me for dear life as I try to squirm away. Mom with this half-smiling, half-terrified look on her face, like, "What have I gotten myself into?" A Polaroid of her and me at what must be the beach in Fort Lauderdale that has 3/82 penciled on the border, just after the separation. Is that why we'd gone? To get away from the suddenly empty house, so she could confide in and be comforted by Grandma? And yet she's smiling. Her eyes are hidden by oversize sunglasses but the smile doesn't look forced.

She's also smiling in the snapshot where she's holding Patchie, this silver scarf covering her head. It's the only picture I've ever seen of her from that time, the only one that exists. It's the most beautiful she's ever looked.

ACKNOWLEDGMENTS

Eternal gratitude to Jim Fitzgerald, Brett Valley, Carrie Thornton, and especially Philip Patrick for enabling this book; to Dad, J., D., and the rest of the family—N. included—for their encouragement and help filling in the gaps; and to V., without whose love I'd never have been able to endure.